practical
floristry

Ring 'A' Roses
FLORIST
106 Market Street
St. Andrews, KY16 9PB
Tel: (0334) 73432
Also at: 18 High Street, Leven
Tel: (0333) 426623

KT-568-240

practical
floristry

Hodder & Stoughton

A MEMBER OF THE HODDER HEADLINE GROUP

British Library Cataloguing in Publication Data

Interflora
   Practical Floristry
   1 Title
   745.92

ISBN 0 340 56940 9 (UK edition)

First published 1992
Impression number 10 9 8 7 6 5 4 3
Year   1998 1997 1996 1995 1994 1993

In the UK

  INTERFLORA is a registered trade mark of Interflora Inc

  The Mercury Man Device is a registered trade mark of Florists Transworld Delivery Association

In other territories

  INTERFLORA is a trade mark of Interflora Inc

  The Mercury Man Device is a trade mark of Florists Transworld Delivery Association

---

Copyright © 1992 Interflora (British Unit) Ltd.

All rights reserved. No part of this publication may be reproduced or transmitted in any form or by any means, electronic or mechanical, including photocopy, recording, or any information storage and retrieval system, without permission in writing from the publisher or under licence from the Copyright Licensing Agency Limited. Further details of such licences (for reprographic reproduction) may be obtained from the Copyright Licensing Agency Limited, of 90 Tottenham Court Road, London W1P 9HE.

Typeset by Wearset, Boldon, Tyne and Wear.
Printed in Hong Kong for the educational publishing division of Hodder & Stoughton Ltd, Mill Road, Dunton Green, Sevenoaks, Kent TNI3 2YA by Colorcraft Ltd.

Contents

Acknowledgments

Interflora wish to thank the following contributors for the long and detailed job of compiling this training manual:

Ken Neighbour – NDSF, Interflora Judges Diploma

Albert Bailey – Interflora Judges Diploma, C & G Teaching Certificate

Irene Bough – NDSF, Interflora Judges Diploma

Betty Jones – NDSF, Past President of Society of Floristry

Lynda Owen – NDSF, Interflora Judges Diploma, C & G Teaching Certificate

Jean Siviter – Interflora Judges Diploma, Diploma of Education

We thank Harry Ware for editing the text and Virginia Kelsey-Wood from our Training Department for co-ordinating the contributions and preparing the final copy.

We acknowledge with thanks, the assistance given by Sylvia Aston, Hazel Bushell, Pat Godwin and Maureen Ockenden and the assistance so freely given by other Interflora Members.

We would like to thank Florists Transworld Delivery (FTD) for allowing us the use of 'In Living Colour' and Interflora Services Plc for allowing us to use transparencies from 'The Collection 1989/90'.

Special thanks to Kate Simunek for the beautifully drawn illustrations, and to Eileen Nott for supplying us with her floristry tools for plate 1. Thank you to everyone concerned, on behalf of the Interflora British Unit.

PRACTICAL FLORISTRY

*F*oreword

Interflora is a very long established Association and the relay service forming the basis of Interflora's business is built on trust and co-operation between Members. The Members also have a strong tradition of self-help and support and have been running floristry training for many years, including providing the *Interflora Floristry Training Manual* throughout the Association.

It is through friendly relationships and mutual help of this kind that the 'family atmosphere' of Interflora has developed, where the experienced and successful help new Members to learn and prosper.

It is with great pleasure that Interflora now feel able to extend a helping hand to all those studying for qualifications in floristry through this book – *Practical Floristry: The Interflora Training Manual.*

Those who have contributed to this book are among the most esteemed in our organisation and their collective wisdom will be of great value to anyone hoping to further their career as a florist. I would like to take this opportunity to thank the contributors for the enormous amount of time and effort that they have expended in producing this book, and express my admiration for the depth of their combined knowledge and flair.

To those of you who use this book, I hope that we may one day welcome you into the family of Interflora. Most of all I hope that you will enjoy using the book and learning from the experience of Interflora.

David Longman
President

INTRODUCTION

*I*ntroduction to Practical Floristry: The Interflora Training Manual

The methods and techniques illustrated in this manual are the result of many hours of discussion by a panel of experienced and successful floristry designers. The designs have been chosen for their practicability and economy in both time and cost.

There are many other equally successful methods used by florists on a daily basis, but we hope that you will try, and evaluate, those in our manual.

All the drawings contained within it are sequential and illustrate the text. The colour photographs give an idea of the finished item. They may not, however, directly illustrate the item they accompany.

The contributors have aimed to provide practical guidance through a progressive range of skills and therefore the items within each chapter are arranged

in ascending order of difficulty in order to help you build confidence. The manual would be most effectively used in conjunction with a course of study in a college or shop. It is also a valuable reference book for specific designs as each item can be used independently. However, it is not intended as a 'teach yourself' guide to floristry.

As this manual is designed for commercial florists, additional allied and subsidiary subjects such as sales, shop practice, order taking and customer care are also addressed.

This manual will give guidance to anyone pursuing a career in floristry, whether a trainee in a college or a shop, or a more senior florist who is looking for a source of new ideas and a concise reference book.

practical **viii** *floristry*

The care and conditioning of flowers and foliage

The reputation of a flower shop rests on the freshness of its flowers and the length of time they last in the customer's home. The correct treatment of flowers determines the length of their life, so conditioning the flowers and getting them to drink immediately they arrive is an important job. It is a skill that has to be learnt: how to cut, where to cut, and how to store them, bearing in mind that flowers need more space as they develop from the bud.

When conditioning flowers, work methodically in a tidy area, knowing where the filled containers are to go, whether it be the shop, cooler or another storage area. Wherever the flowers are to be stored, aim for maximum air space and minimum damage. Have clean containers and fresh (preferably tepid) water ready for the flowers. Add cut flower food. It gives flowers longer life and helps to keep the water clear and fresh.

Learn to handle a knife. Observe the rule, 'Safety first not first aid'. Keep your knife in first class order. A blunt knife is more dangerous than a sharp one.

Handle flower stems carefully and prevent damage. Save any broken flower heads for the workroom. Do not have a total loss through breakage. From each stem take off any green leaves that may come below water level. Green leaves decay in water and set up bacterial action which clogs the cells, destroys the stems and prevents water being taken up.

Using your clean, sharp knife, cut the stem ends diagonally to open up the maximum number of stem cells to take up water. Delicate, less tolerant flowers and those needed urgently for orders and the workroom must go into water first.

Flowers arriving in a very soft condition should have their stem ends cut and be left in their market wraps to drink and straighten. They can be prepared for shop sale later. Any limp flowers should also be wrapped and put aside to drink and straighten.

Every member of staff must recognise when flowers in any part of the shop are not drinking so that they can be recut immediately under warm water. All that is needed is a moment of skilled time to rescue a flower in the early stages of dehydration. It may well recover completely.

Throw away decaying material every day. The decaying process produces Ethylene gas that kills nearby flowers. Box all rubbish. Leave your work area clean; work surfaces wiped and the floor swept.

The economic way to unpack and handle flowers

Unpacking and handling flowers when they arrive at your shop is a task which calls for skill and economy. Learn the different ways flowers are packaged for market and handle them deftly so that stems and flower heads are not damaged or broken.

By handling flowers you learn the crisp feel and bright look of fresh material and soon recognise the jaded look and limp feel of older flowers.

When you are handling or conditioning flowers let your boss know when you come across any flowers which are of very good or very poor quality. In the event of them being inferior the market can be contacted for a refund and future buying adapted. This exchange of information keeps flower wastage down and profitability up.

When unpacking you may be responsible for checking the quantities of flowers against the invoice. Make a note on the invoice of any differences and notify the boss. Make sure that your shop pays only for the flowers delivered.

Every day there will be a list of flowers which have been bought for specified gift orders and special make-up work. Check that they have arrived, label them, and put them aside so that no one touches them.

You handle the flowers as they arrive and so have the most up to date knowledge of what varieties are available for sale. Other staff rely on you for such information.

Unpacking soon teaches you the names and varieties of flowers and foliages. It lays the foundation of your floristry vocabulary. The responsibility of the job is a major step towards understanding the floristry trade.

The economy of stock rotation

Correct stock rotation is basic to a shop's economy and reputation. Every shop must have a standard drill of where and how to store flowers in their correct day rotation. Date labelling is wise.

The day's flowers that need a long drink before being sold must be stored in a position secondary to those that have already been conditioned.

Tender flowers with a short vase life must be moved quickly through the rotation.

Flowers that arrive in good, but open conditions have to be recognised and moved forward early. This calls for skilled judgement of quality and condition. Have a word with the boss.

The aim of a flower shop is to get flowers into a customer's home and to have them last a long time. No mature flowers must find their way into the order packing area. At their peak of opening, flowers must be put aside for funeral work, where they will be seen in all their loveliness.

It is the duty of every member of staff to know exactly what flowers are in the shop, their quality, condition, and location. No one should go around with their eyes shut. The proper movement of flowers through the shop and the observation of that movement is everyone's responsibility.

The profitability and good name of a flower shop depends on proper stock rotation.

Note. For further information about care and conditioning refer to tables 2–4 in appendix 1.

Foliage

There are two distinct types of foliage coming through a florist's shop:

- The tough foliage used in funeral work needs water to maintain its crisp, green texture so that it looks well in the tribute. Its stems are often woody and if a knife is not strong enough to cut them, the ends should be crushed before putting them into water.

- Choice foliage, especially the cultivated varieties, must be cut diagonally with a knife, maybe on two sides of the stem to expose the maximum number of cells to drink. Elegant foliage stems can be put aside for shop sales and orders.

Foliage is appreciated and commands a good price. Knowledge and sureness of the value of foliage can up-grade window displays, enhance the appeal of gift designs and greatly assist profitability.

Plant care

Plant care plays an important part in the economy of many florists' shops. To reduce the risk of high wastage, a knowledge of plants' requirements is essential. Ideally, one person should be responsible for plant welfare in a shop. This way an extensive knowledge of the plant stocks held by the shop is built up and their sales can be developed.

Stock coming into the shop must be checked for inventory quality and condition.

First check the plant's label for instructions on its care

When unpacking and handling plants, learn to observe their condition. Remove any debris from the surface of the compost; clean the pots with a damp cloth and check the labels. The larger and more expensive plants must be individually labelled, clearly and correctly (with their names spelt accurately) and their retail price.

If damage is only slight, broken plants can be trimmed and tidied. Shortages and serious defects should be reported immediately.

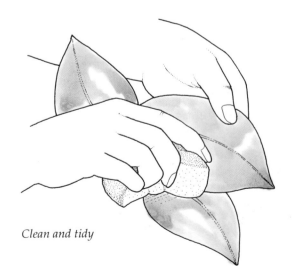

Clean and tidy

Trim

Generally, shop conditions are not ideal for keeping plants in good condition and understanding their basic needs will help you to maintain them more effectively. All green plants rely on four essentials in their correct proportions, if they are to thrive. Those requirements are:

- Light,
- Moisture,
- Air, and
- Temperature,

all of which interact with each other.

Light

Plants arriving in closed boxes must be opened immediately to expose them to natural light. Plant sleeves should be removed or slackened to allow air to circulate freely and, again, to allow maximum light to reach them.

These first requirements are vital, because some plants will deteriorate rapidly in dark, airless conditions. An attractive display to promote sales is very important, but the natural light in many shops is inadequate to support many types of plants. So, learn to observe the quality of light within the available display space in the shop. Allocate the available areas to the various groups of plants according to their degree of tolerance. Plants with large, leathery leaves, like *Ficus plastica* (rubber plant), for example, are more tolerant of inadequate lighting than the smaller leaved variegated types, like the *Chlorophytum* (spider plant) varieties.

Arrange your display with this in mind. Change it often so that plants are rotated through areas which have good light. Keep their leaves clean and dust free. Flowering plants must be displayed in well-lit positions to keep them in peak condition.

Moisture

In your shop you may stock large and medium specimen plants which are used mainly for display and sell rather slowly and smaller foliage and flowering plants which need to be prominently displayed for quick and regular sales.

The first group may need extra care in their maintenance because the loss of even one plant due to neglect can result in a serious financial set-back. Over-watering a plant, even once, can do irreparable harm. The most reliable way of assessing plants' watering requirements, is by their weight. Compare one with another in a given batch when you are handling them. Relative lightness in the weight of a plant denotes dryness. In poor conditions with poor light, little water will be needed. It may be better to give them only enough water to keep the compost from drying out completely.

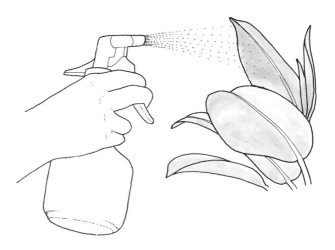

In good light, with summer temperatures you may need to soak the plant. Do so by submerging the pot completely, but *make sure the plant is thoroughly drained before placing it in an outer container.* Leaving a plant to stand too long in even a little water is almost always fatal. Modern composts have good porosity and are designed to drain freely and yet retain moisture. Air at the roots is essential for a plant to remain healthy and thrive. Too much water excludes the essential oxygen from the compost and the roots very soon sicken and die, causing leaves to turn yellow or develop brown, dried-up edges or patches. Many types shed their leaves altogether. Plastic pots are not porous and the compost in them dries out slowly, so watering calls for extra care.

A water sprayer is an essential tool for plant care. Regular misting over the leaves of most foliage plants, especially in warm weather, will keep the plants looking fresh and reduce the need for further watering. During summer time add foliage feed to the sprayer as an extra boost. As a general rule do not spray over plants with furry leaves or those which are in flower.

Temperature

Most plants thrive in temperatures around 65–70° F (17–20° C), and growth begins to slow down when temperatures fall below about 55° F (13° C). Draughts are detrimental to plants left on the floor, where temperatures are lower and damage will occur.

Weekends in a flower shop can be hazardous for plants. Take time before you leave to check water requirements carefully. Place the plants where they can benefit from the available light without exposing them to full sunlight or extremes of temperature, the shop windows for example. No plants should be left on the floor where they will be exposed to draughts and above all, do not leave them standing in water.

Air

Plants thrive in fresh air, free from draughts, so space them so that they benefit from the free circulation of air. Fungal diseases, like *Botrytis*, develop in stagnant conditions and low temperatures.

Feeding

Modern composts contain fertilizers which are released regularly over a prescribed period, according to the needs of the plant, this can vary from six weeks to almost a year. So except for semi-permanent

displays the florist need not be concerned about feeding the plants. However, point out to your customers that plants need to be fed during the summer. This will give you the opportunity to make an additional sale of plant food.

If you remember that light, temperature and water requirements are interdependent in plant care and act accordingly you will reduce wastage and sell a better product.

The florist's tool box

Floristry scissors*
Ribbon scissors*
Secateurs*
Pocket knife*
Large blade foam cutting knife*
Sellotape
Pot tape, narrow and wide for economical use –
    green and white
Wreath wrap
Binding tape for fine work, green and white
String, raffia or plastic ties for tied assemblies
Corsage pins
German pins
Staple gun and staples
Glue gun and glue
Tissues
Tissue paper
Hand towel
Polythene sheeting
Mossing reel wire
Wires, support wire and stub wires –
    basic and covered
'Wire tidy' to keep wires conveniently in gauges
    and protect from wet work benches
Water spray/mister
Waterproof plasters

* All to be kept well sharpened

See Plate 1

Use of a glue gun

The glue gun is an electrical device which takes a stick of solid glue, melts it to a liquid form and pushes the hot, liquid glue through a nozzle, usually by means of a trigger control, to the desired spot. The glue is very hot and quickly solidifies.

Almost any material in common use by florists can be stuck by this useful and very versatile piece of equipment: flowers, ribbon, foam and almost everything else. When the glue hardens, most substances are firmly fixed, *provided* they were dry when the hot glue was applied.

If the glue gun is used with care, it is a marvellous tool for the busy florist, but care must be taken. *Hot glue can burn the skin severely*. Should this happen, place the affected part in cold water immediately.

NB.   ALL ELECTRICAL EQUIPMENT MUST BE KEPT AWAY FROM WATER. DISCONNECT YOUR GLUE GUN WHEN IT IS NOT IN USE. CHECK WIRING REGULARLY.

There are many types of glue gun, varying from inexpensive models in which the glue stick is pushed through the gun manually, to more expensive and sophisticated models with a trigger action, heat and light controls. Glue sticks are usually sold by weight. Use only sufficient glue to stick the material securely. Too much glue results in an untidy finish.

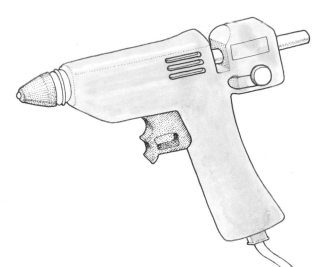

GIFT PACKAGING

*I*ntroduction

Most of our flower sales are for gifts, many of them delivered directly to the recipients. When they are received, their impact should be immediate.

Distinctive packaging will not only enhance the flowers, it will also protect them. With a host of packaging materials to choose from, stunning gift wrapped designs can be achieved with a few basic techniques and ideas.

Today's customers are professional consumers. They are discerning and expect sleek, attractive presentation. The value of distinctive packaging cannot be over-emphasised. It influences a customer's decision on whether or not to buy, particularly with impulse sales.

Gift packaging can be as simple or elaborate as the cost dictates. It can be developed to enhance your shop's reputation for giving a discerning service to its customers but, whatever the method of packaging used, the basic rules of good floristry must apply.

Always use a good selection of fresh, top quality flowers and foliage, well conditioned and suitable for the occasion. Choose them carefully for their shape, colour and fragrance. Use smart, clean packaging materials with crisp decoration and finish the gift wrap with a neatly written gift card and envelope. Do not forget the care card and flower food.

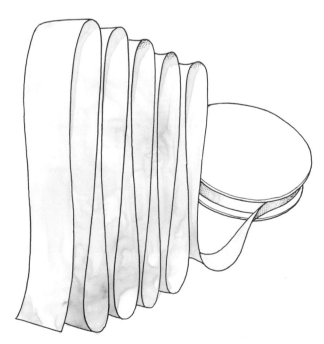

Fig. 2.1

*B*ows

Most florists will demonstrate their particular method of making a bow for a gift pack. All of them are perfectly good, tried and tested and they all vary in their complexity. But perhaps the simplest and most convenient is the flat bow, which is easy to store and can be made up in a range of colours when there is a moment to spare in the shop. At peak periods, when time is at a premium, a stock of ready made bows, instantly available, is invaluable.

METHOD

1 From a roll of 2" wide tearable ribbon, cut some 26" (650 mm) lengths and tear them into strips ¼" (6 mm) wide. These will form the ties to secure the bows to the gift packs.

2 With the ribbon still attached to the roll, pull off a length and every 9" (225 mm) fold it onto itself until five 9" loops are formed. If a larger bow is required more loops can be added (*Fig. 2.1*).

3 Fold the series of 9" loops in two, so that you have all the loops at one end and the central tying point at the other (*Fig. 2.2*).

4 On either side of this point make diagonal cuts to within ⅛" (3 mm) of the centre line. This will result in two 'V' shaped cuts, opposite each other, on either side of the ribbon, separated by ¼" (6 mm) of uncut ribbon (*Fig. 2.3*).

5 Tie at this point, using one of the ¼" (6 mm) strips.

6 It is in this form that the bow is stored.

7 When required, tie to the gift pack, encircling it with the ties, and knot it immediately above the bow.
The loops can then be pulled out and teased into a pleasing bow with a little practice.

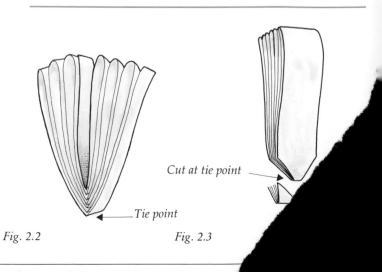

Cut at tie point

Tie point

Fig. 2.2   *Fig. 2.3*

R*ose in a box*

Single flowers presented in gift wrapping or a presentation box are very popular with the general public. Of these, a single rose is probably the most popular, for obvious reasons. Over the years, the red rose has become a symbol of love. To give a single red rose has become a romantic and symbolic gesture. Other colours of rose, and other flowers are also popular.

The Interflora rose box is specially designed to hold a small bottle of water to keep the flower from premature wilting. The boxes are packed flat and assembled by the florist when required.

MATERIALS

A well conditioned, perfect rose.
A piece of foliage, asparagus fern, for example.

SUNDRIES

Rose box in two flat pieces (liner and outer box)
Bottle
Sellotape
Ribbon to decorate

METHOD

1 Start with a clean, dry work surface.

2 Make up the box carefully, folding it without creasing or causing damage.

3 Fold the gold liner into position.

4 Half fill the bottle with water, fit it into the liner, and replace the rubber cap. Do not over-fill the bottle or water will spill out and damage the box when the rose stem is inserted into it.

5 Make sure the bottle is dry before placing it in the box.

6 Only the best flower should be chosen for a single rose presentation. Examine it carefully, making sure there is no damage or bruising of the petals or foliage.

7 Measure the rose against the inner box. There must be space between the rose and the lid. A rose pushing onto the lid will become damaged and bruised. The flower should be shown to its best advantage.

8 Cut the stem on a slant and push it through the rubber top of the bottle. A piece of foliage, such as fern, can be added if required. When the foliage on the rose is poor, or, some leaves have to be removed, additional foliage is essential.

9 If necessary, the holes in the lining can be used to secure the rose to the liner with ribbon. A bow can be added on the lower ribbon ties if required.

10 From the top, slide the liner with the rose into the outer box. Fold in the top lid to fit.

11 Secure the base with a piece of Sellotape for added security.

12 The outer box can be decorated with ribbon, picks etc. as appropriate.

13 Attach a care card, greetings card and envelope and a guarantee card in a suitable position.

See Plate 2

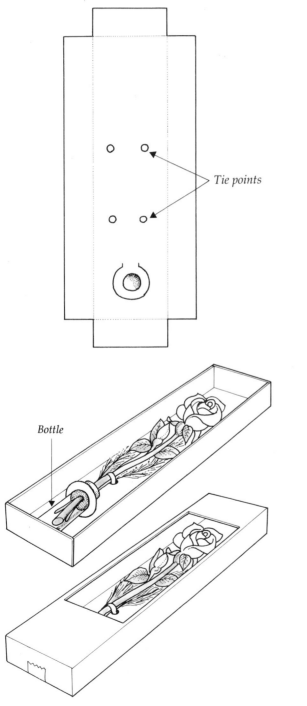

Tie points

Bottle

GIFT PACKAGING

Single flower in a cylinder

One of the florist's more popular gift designs is the single flower in a clear PVC cylinder. The cylinders are a very versatile medium for the busy florist. They are available in a variety of sizes, some printed or embossed with a motif, others plain. They can accommodate a single flower or several. Being quick and easy to assemble, cylinders are a very valuable asset at peak periods and, perhaps their greatest virtue, they are suitable for any gift occasion.

In a single flower format, the cylinder is relatively inexpensive, hence its popularity with many of our customers.

There are several methods of assembling a single flower cylinder presentation. Perhaps the simplest and quickest comprises a small bottle of water with a soft rubber cap. The sharpened flower stem is pushed through the cap, into the water, and both are gently lowered into the cylinder. An alternative method is shown below:

——— MATERIALS ———

One perfect single flower, such as a rose or carnation (a carnation is illustrated but a rose is perhaps, more popular) and a piece of unblemished foliage, such as asparagus fern or eucalyptus.

SUNDRIES

A cylinder, with lid
A round piece of foam
2″ (50 mm) wide ribbon
Ribbon to decorate
Sellotape
Guarantee and care card
Greetings card and envelope
Cellofilm

METHOD

1 Start with a clean, dry bench.

2 Soak the round of foam, taking care not to over-soak it.

3 Select the required flower and stem of foliage, ensuring that neither is damaged or blemished.

4 Cut a piece of cellofilm, large enough to cover the sides of the foam. Wrap it tightly around the sides of the foam and secure it with Sellotape. Take a piece of Sellotape across the bottom of the foam, securing it onto the cellofilm at either side. This will prevent the inside of the cylinder becoming smeared when the foam is pushed into the cylinder (*Fig. 2.4*).

Wrap Cellofilm around the side of the foam to prevent smearing when sliding foam into cylinder

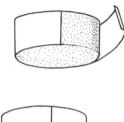

Fig. 2.4   Secure film to base with Sellotape ensuring join is at the back of design

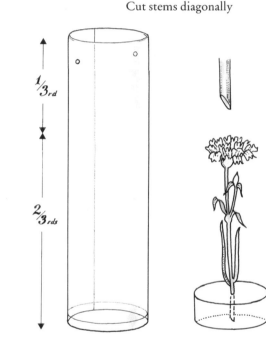

Cut stems diagonally

$\frac{1}{3}^{rd}$

$\frac{2}{3}^{rds}$

Fig. 2.5

5 Place the soaked foam on the bench with the cylinder beside it. Using the height of the cylinder as a guide, diagonally cut the flower stem to two thirds of the height of the cylinder (*Fig. 2.5*).

6 Insert the flower stem into the foam, pushing it well in to ensure that it is firmly and securely anchored (*Fig. 2.5*).

7 Insert the foliage into the foam behind the flower. Use the diameter of the cylinder as a guide to the correct 'spread' of the foliage. Too much foliage will result in a cluttered look once the design is placed inside the cylinder.

8 Decorate the top of the foam with a neat ribbon bow, taking care to select a colour which will complement the flowers (*Fig. 2.6*).

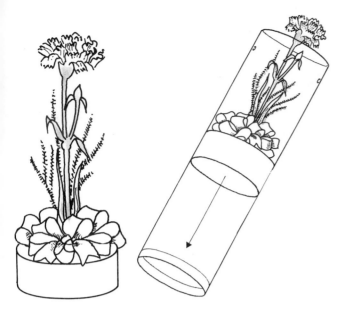

Fig. 2.6   Fig. 2.7

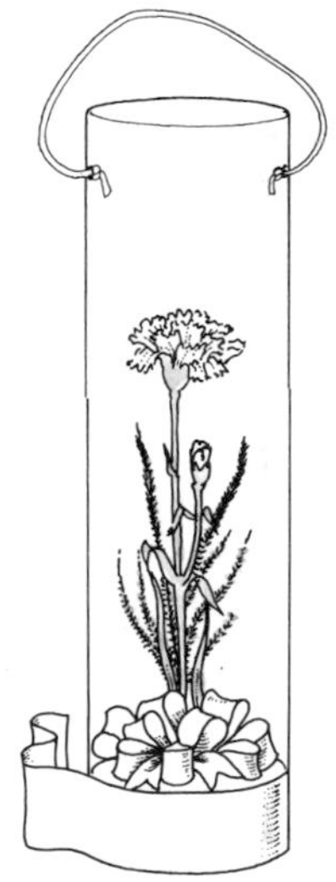

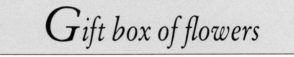

*M*ulti flower cylinder presentation

Following a very similar method and using the same techniques, the single flower cylinder can be developed into a multi flower presentation.

It is suggested that three carnations be used and the following method followed:

METHOD

1 The first placement is cut to approximately three quarters the length of the cylinder.

2 The second placement should measure approximately half the length of the cylinder.

3 The third placement should be cut short to be recessed almost to the top surface of the foam.

4 To assemble, follow the same method as that used in the single flower cylinder presentation.

See Plate 3

Fig. 2.8 Secure ribbon at the rear of cylinder

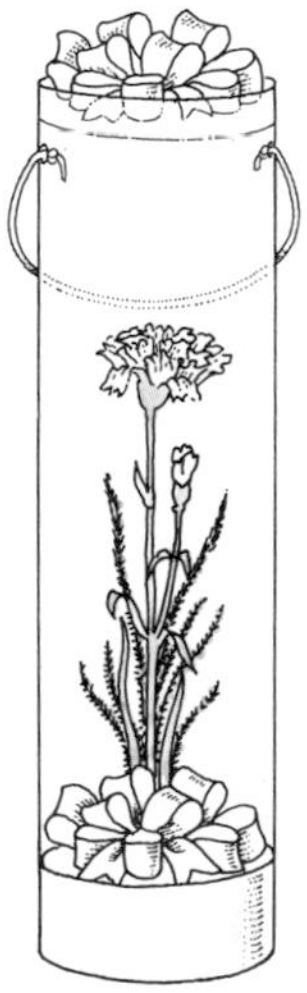

Fig. 2.9 Finish cylinder off with a bow

9 Carefully slide the foam into the cylinder, making sure that the join in the cylinder is to the rear of the design (*Fig. 2.7*).

10 Cover the base of the cylinder with a 2″ (50 mm) ribbon to conceal the foam and secure it with glue. The join should be to the rear of the cylinder (*Fig. 2.8*).

11 The cylinder comes complete with a short length of gilt cord. Thread it through the holes at the top of the cylinder to form a handle (*Fig. 2.9*).

12 Fix the lid to the cylinder with Sellotape.

13 Decorate the exterior of the cylinder with narrow ribbon and a bow.

14 Attach the guarantee and greetings card, in its envelope, to the cylinder.

*G*ift box of flowers

A gift box of flowers makes an attractive and luxurious present, ideally suited to every gift occasion as an alternative to a bouquet of flowers.

Gift boxes can be supplied in a number of sizes. Some makes can be printed with your shop's name, if required. They have a number of advantages, particularly in saving space. When delivered they are packed flat for convenient storage.

Boxed flowers are extremely well protected from damage in transit and, at peak periods, the completed boxes can be stacked in the van to save space. Attach cards and envelopes to one end of the boxes so that they are easily seen. Most types of flowers are suitable for gift boxes, but care must be taken when selecting them. The length of the box will determine the length of stem. Very long stems are unsuitable for smaller boxes; much of the stem would have to be cut off for the flowers to fit inside them.

MATERIALS

Spray carnations, spring flowers, carnations, freesia, cymbidium orchid sprays, roses and many others.

Foliages should be light to enhance the flowers. Eucalyptus, leather leaf, asparagus fern and pittosporum are suggested.

SUNDRIES

Gift box, assembled in accordance with the manufacturer's instructions
Ribbon
Sellotape
Care and greetings cards and envelope
Flower food

METHOD

1 Ensure the bench is clean and dry.

2 Assemble the box according to the manufacturer's instructions, taking care not to crease or damage it.

3 Select the flowers and foliage.

4 If a liner is supplied with the box, thread a tying ribbon through the holes provided at the tying point. Replace the liner and arrange the flowers within the box (*Fig. 2.10*).

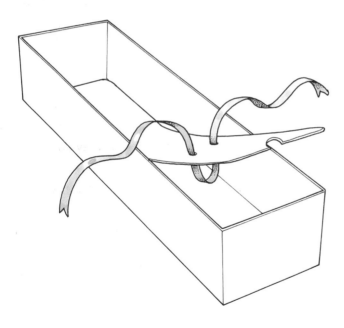

Fig. 2.10   Attach ribbon to card tie points

5 If no liner is supplied, arrange the flowers in the box and tie them below the focal area.

6 When arranging the flowers in the box, leave the stems as long as possible. Arrange them to reveal as many flowers as possible, visible through the acetate window in the lid. Finish with the smaller, choicer flowers lower down, towards the tying point. Tie the stems at the tying point, underneath the focal flowers. Attach a bow to cover the tying material.

7 Place a sachet of flower food in the box, together with the care card.

8 Close the box and secure the lid neatly with Sellotape at both ends.

9 Attach the card, in its envelope to one end of the box, where it can be seen easily (*Fig. 2.11*).

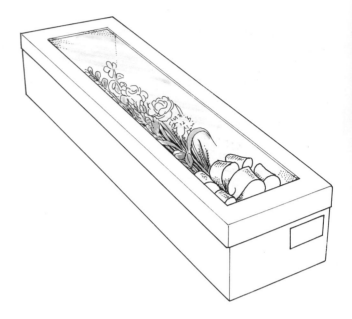

Fig. 2.11   Secure card and envelope to the box

10 Decorate the outside of the box.

See Plate 4

Gift wrapping a pot plant

Even the smallest plant can be transformed into a seemingly more expensive and special gift. Gift wrapping does more than enhance the appearance of a plant, it protects it from damage and adverse weather. Some plants are delicate. Completely enclosing them in cellofilm provides them with essential protection. Gift wrapping should be done speedily if a customer is waiting in the shop.

There are a variety of ways of gift wrapping a plant but which ever method you follow always ensure that you use sufficient cellofilm to avoid crushing and damaging the plant. The amount of cellofilm you use, of course, will depend upon the size of the plant you are gift wrapping.

MATERIALS

A good quality plant in a 5″ (125 mm) pot (approx.).

SUNDRIES

Cellofilm (Cellocoup, for example), sufficient for the size of plant to be wrapped
Sellotape
Ribbon
Care card
Greetings card and envelope

METHOD

1 Make sure the bench is clean and dry.

2 Choose a good, undamaged, healthy plant.

3 Ensure that the pot is clean and remove the price label.

4 Cut a piece of cellofilm to the size of the plant plus approximately 15" (375 mm) and lie it flat on the bench (*Fig. 2.12*).

Fig. 2.12

5 Taking care not to damage it, lie the plant on its side, on the cellofilm, facing the top left hand corner.

6 Bring the bottom left hand corner of the cellofilm loosely over the plant in line diagonally with the top right hand corner. Start to roll the cellofilm and plant to begin to form a cone shape (*Fig. 2.13a*). Before the

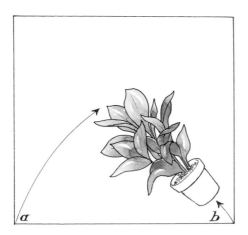

Fig. 2.13

cone is complete fold the bottom of the cellofilm upwards (*Fig. 2.13b*) and continue the rolling action until a neat cone is formed. Secure with a small piece of Sellotape at the base of the plant pot.

7 Fold the top flap of cellofilm over the plant to enclose it. Secure with Sellotape or Interflora sticker and decorate with ribbon (*Fig. 2.14*).

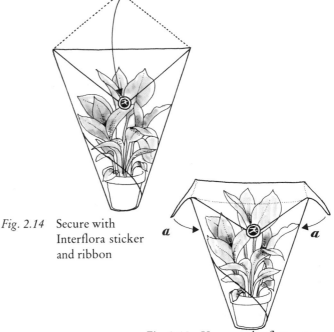

Fig. 2.14   Secure with Interflora sticker and ribbon

Fig. 2.15   Very gently, flatten top

8 Carefully flatten the top of the cellofilm, avoiding damage to the plant (*Fig. 2.15*).

9 Fold the two end points downwards, creasing the folds to give a crisp, straight edge (Fig. 2.15a).

10 Sellotape the corners neatly on each side.

11 This method will produce a tidy and symmetrical, square or rectangular top surface to the gift wrapping (*Fig. 2.16*).

Fig. 2.16

12 Attach the care card, gift card and envelope.

GIFT PACKAGING

Gift wrapping

Gift wrapping flowers not only enhances their appearance, it makes them look special and protects them from the weather and accidental damage. Furthermore, when the stems are completely enclosed, transpiration is reduced to a minimum and the risk of premature wilting is lessened considerably.

There are many ways of gift wrapping flowers. The quantity and size of flowers and foliages will determine the size of the finished gift bouquet. Before starting a gift wrap, check the order. Are there any specific instructions regarding colour and flower content?

Does the card message give any clues to the nature of the occasion? This will often help the florist to choose flowers which are appropriate. It may also give an indication of what the customer is expecting.

Is the order being made up for the correct date?

The message on the card is often more important than the flowers, so it is essential that it is neatly written on a clean card. Has the spelling been checked?

MATERIALS

When selecting flowers, customer satisfaction must be uppermost in your mind. Colour, lasting qualities, the shapes of flowers and their perfume are all important considerations. With this in mind, the following flowers are suggested:

Flowers for length: eg. iris, gladioli, liatris, larkspur
For value: eg. spray carnations and spray chrysanthemums
Choice flowers: eg. carnations, lilies, roses, alstroemeria
Small focal flowers: eg. freesia, Singapore orchids
Foliage: the foliage you choose should be light and enhance the flowers: eg. eucalyptus, leather leaf, asparagus fern and pittosporum are suggested.

SUNDRIES

Cellofilm (eg. Cellocoup)
Ribbon to tone with the flowers and cellofilm
Stapler and staples
Tying tape eg. Cellotwist
Greetings card and envelope
Sachet of flower food
Scissors and sharp knife

METHOD

There are many methods of making a gift wrap, the one shown here is for a small bouquet.

1 The workbench must be clean and dry.

2 Select flowers and foliage and place them in a vase on the workbench until required.

3 Take sufficient cellofilm to cover the entire length of the flowers and foliage plus an additional 12″ (300 mm). Lay it on the workbench, making sure that the lettering and ornamental design on the wrapping are facing down onto the bench, so that when the gift wrap is complete the design is on the correct side (*Fig. 2.17*).

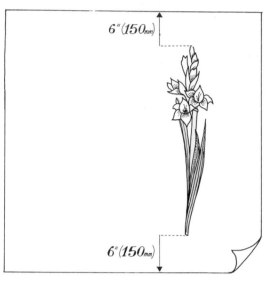

6″ *(150mm)*

6″ *(150mm)*

Fig. 2.17 Cut your Cellocoup to the length of the longest flower plus 12″ (300 mm)

4 Start by placing flowers and foliage on either the left or right hand side of the Cellocoup. The taller ones first, towards the top of the gift wrap, then graduating the shorter stems towards the bottom.

5 Any delicate flowers which may damage easily should be placed towards the centre of the gift wrap for added protection. Group flowers through the design to create pleasing patterns of shape and colour. Ensure that no flowers are crushed or concealed by others.

6 Tie all the stems together securely under the focal point to prevent them becoming dislodged. Sometimes the stems are long enough to pass through the tying point without the need to tie them inside the gift wrap. They will be secured by the exterior tie which is made in the final stages, but whichever method is followed, no stems must be left loose to float around inside the gift wrap when it is complete.

7 Trim only those stems which are of extreme length.

8 The tied flowers and foliage are now lying on one side of the cellofilm. Close the wrap by bringing the other side over the flowers and form a hem on the underside. Staple neatly along its entire length (*Fig. 2.18*).

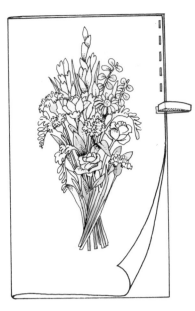

Fig. 2.18 Position flowers on one half of Cellocoup. Fold other half over to the opposite edge

Fig. 2.20 Gather Cellocoup at the tie point and attach bow

9 Form a hem and staple along the bottom of the wrap (*Fig. 2.19*).

12 Attach a sachet of flower food with a staple or short piece of Sellotape near the bow.

13 Enclose the card in a clearly addressed envelope and staple or Sellotape to the gift wrap, taking care not to deface the card.

See Plates 5 and 5a

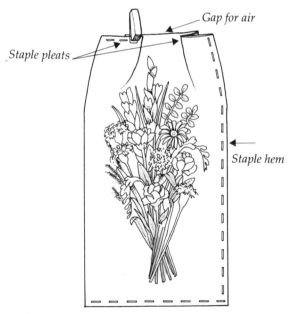

Fig. 2.19

10 At the top, make a neat pleat either side of the centre and staple. This leaves a small opening in the centre of the gift wrap to allow air to circulate, thus reducing misting of the cellofilm. Alternatively, the top of the gift wrap can be hemmed and stapled.

11 Attach a bow neatly and securely in a position over the tying point (*Fig.2.20*).

Hand tied bouquet

Hand tied bouquets are arrangements which are made in the hand, with flowers and foliage firmly tied together when the bouquet is finished. One of the advantages of a hand tied bouquet is that the whole design can be placed in a vase of water without untying it. **(See Plates 6 and 6a.)**

Hand tied bouquets can be as simple or elaborate as the price or occasion dictates. They can be made in a variety of shapes, sizes and styles, both front facing and all round. The flowers in this type of design last well because the stems can drink more easily than flowers in foam, and the water can be changed without disturbing the arrangement. So hand tied bouquets are ideal gifts to send to hospitals, for presentations and, in fact, for almost any gift occasion.

A vase is integral to this design and presents the florist with an ideal opportunity for a supplementary sale.

Fig. 2.21   *Fig. 2.22*

Fig. 2.23

MATERIALS

Almost any flowers and foliage can be used in this type of design. If using mixed flowers, choose them carefully for their shape, colour and texture. Foliage plays an important role in hand tied bouquets. Bushy foliage, such as fern and eucalyptus help to achieve an open design. For this example, the following flowers have been chosen: carnations, roses, spray carnations and gypsophila. And for foliage: tree ivy or any other inexpensive, bushy foliage; eucalyptus; leather leaf; bear grass.

SUNDRIES

Raffia, tying ribbon or other such material will also be required to secure the bouquet.

For gift wrapping:
Cellocoup and Cellotwist
Greeting card and envelope
Ribbon of a complementary colour and,
A sachet of flower food.

METHOD

1 Place flowers and foliage in groups on a clean, dry work surface so that they can easily be picked up.

2 Defoliate and clean all stems which will be below the tying point. Tease out and prepare gypsophila and foliage.

3 Spiralling the stems of all the flowers around the focal flower is an essential element of this design. It is achieved by inserting the front flowers from left to right, and those at the rear from right to left. One of your hands is your 'container' with the thumb and first finger used to hold the bouquet.

4 Start with a small bunch of tree ivy and add some taller pieces of eucalyptus (*Fig. 2.21*).

5 Add the flowers, starting with a carnation placed vertically in the centre and following with additional carnations, inserted as described in point 3 (*Fig. 2.22*).

6 Keep adding the gypsophila and eucalyptus between the flowers to act as a cushion between the stems and keep the flowers in the required position. Cushioning with bushy foliage also helps to give the bouquet an open, loose appearance.

7 Add roses next, maintaining them in a prominent position and forming a circular outline. Thread the stems through the foliage and gypsophila by relaxing the hand slightly. Make sure the rose stems are long enough to maintain them in a prominent position. If they have been pushed too far into the design they will not give the required impact.

8 Add the spray carnations around the edge of the bouquet in a circular formation. Keep spiralling the stems.

9 Bear grass, in small bunches of three or four stems, is strategically placed in the design to give 'movement' within the bouquet.

10 Finish off with a collar of leather leaf around the bouquet, just above the tying point (*Fig. 2.23*).

11 To hold the assembled flowers and foliage securely, use sufficient tying ribbon or raffia to go round the stems several times. Double the raffia and pass it round the bouquet at the tying point. Thread the two ends through the loop which has been formed and pull them tight. Separate the ends and pass them round the stems in opposite directions. Tie them together firmly with a double knot. Throughout the tying operation, take care not to allow the raffia to wander from the

Plate 1 Floristry tools

Plate 2 Rose in a box and rose in a cylinder

Plate 3 Multi flower cylinder presentation

Plate 4 Gift box of flowers

tying point. Trim the stem ends on a slant (*Fig. 2.24*). On the finished bouquet, the length of stem below the tying point should be approximately one third that of the finished bouquet (*Fig. 2.25*).

Fig. 2.24

2/3rds

1/3rd

Fig. 2.25

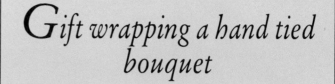

*G*ift wrapping a hand tied bouquet

Flowers need protection from the weather and from handling after they leave your shop. Wrapping them in cellofilm, not only protects the flowers, it glamorises them and gives a more luxurious effect.

There are many ways of gift wrapping a hand tied bouquet. The method to use will depend upon the size of the bouquet, its shape and the occasion for which it is required.

The method shown is a simple cone wrap which is gathered at the tying point to give the required width without crushing the flowers. Florists should try new and different methods. Experimenting is essential to find the best method.

SUNDRIES

Cellofilm
Ribbon of an appropriate colour
Gift card and envelope
Flower food

METHOD

1 The size of the cellofilm should equal the length of the bouquet plus approximately 6" (150 mm). Place it on a clean, dry work surface (*Fig. 2.26*).

2 Place the bouquet diagonally on the cellofilm. The top of the bouquet should face the top left hand corner of the wrapping (*Fig 2.27*).

6" (150mm)

Fig. 2.26

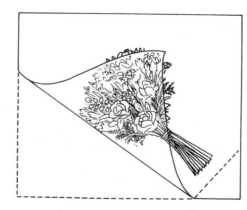

Fig. 2.27   Fold corner over loosely

Fig. 2.28   Gather at tie point

3 Take the bottom left hand corner and bring it loosely over the flowers and hold it in position lightly to avoid damaging them (*Fig. 2.27*).

4 Fold the bottom corner upwards (*Fig. 2.27*) and gently roll the bouquet and its wrapping to form a cone, gathering the cellofilm around the tying point as you do so. This will produce the additional width required for the wrapping to protect the flowers without crushing them (*Fig. 2.28*).

5 Make a bow of a size and colour to enhance the flowers.

6 Attach the ribbon bow by taking the long trails around the tying point and knotting them firmly immediately above the bow (*Fig. 2.29*).

7 If the bouquet requires further embellishment, finish off the gift wrap with a small piece of curled ribbon. Secure it to the top of the cone.

8 The greetings card and its envelope, neatly and clearly written, must be secured to the cellofilm, together with a sachet of flower food.

Fig. 2.29   Corners can be rounded

Alternative method of wrapping

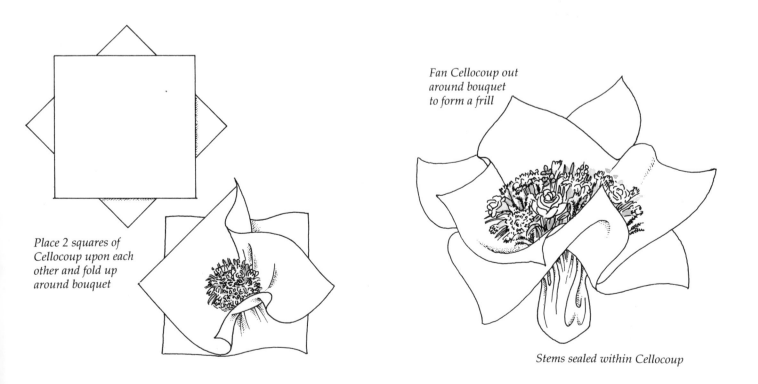

Place 2 squares of Cellocoup upon each other and fold up around bouquet

Fan Cellocoup out around bouquet to form a frill

Stems sealed within Cellocoup

*F*ront facing tied bouquet

A front facing tied bouquet is made in the hand. On completion, the stems are tied together, and the bouquet can be placed in a vase without further rearrangement. The design resembles an arrangement and can be made in several different styles, symmetrical, asymmetrical or a modern design (**See Plate 7.**). A mass of flowers can be used or just one or two choice blooms. The choice of design will often be dictated by the style of vase to be used.

Although the design is front facing, some materials must be placed at the back of the bouquet if the correct balance, both visual and actual, is to be achieved. The bouquet will not sit correctly in the vase if it is not properly balanced, and it will fall forward.

—————— MATERIALS ——————

Flowers and foliage must be selected carefully if the desired effect is to be attained. The important considerations when choosing them are shape, colour and texture. Foliage is most important in hand tied bouquets to give width and depth to the design. The following examples of flowers are suggested:
Upright flowers: gladioli, liatris, nanus, bullrushes and larkspur
Choice flowers: roses, gerberas, carnations and freesias
Flowers to fill the base of the design: statice, hydrangea heads, alchemilla mollis, spray chrysanthemum heads

The following examples of foliage are suggested:
Foliage for width: large leaves such as *Hosta fatsia*, dieffenbachia, laurel
Trailing foliage: hedera trails, bear grass
Filler foliage: tree ivy, *Viburnum tinus*, eucalyptus

Other interesting materials can be used to advantage. Contorted willow, dried seed heads, larch branches, lilies, molucella, bun moss, alliums and dried grasses are typical examples. Using too many materials will result in a cluttered appearance, the art of good design relies upon the selection and limitation of the materials used.

SUNDRIES

Tying tape or raffia, a suitable vase

METHOD

1 Place the flowers and foliage on a clean, dry bench in groups so that they can be picked up easily.

2 Defoliate and clean all the stems which will fall below the tying point of the finished bouquet.

3 The stems of all the flowers in a hand tied bouquet should spiral. To make this possible, flowers at the front of the bouquet should be fed in from left to right. Those at the rear should be fed from right to left. Turning the bouquet when necessary and keeping the hand relaxed allows the flowers to be moved and repositioned where necessary.

4 Use one of your hands as a 'container'. Start by taking a small bunch of bushy foliage, *Viburnum tinus*, for example, and hold it in the gap created by the thumb and forefinger of your 'container' hand (*Fig. 2.30*).

Fig. 2.30

Fig. 2.31

5 Using the upright flowers, such as liatris, arrange three of them in a group. Two thirds of the stem length should be above the hand to achieve the desired height (*Fig. 2.31*).

Fig. 2.32

Plates 5 and 5a   Gift wrapped bouquets

Fig. 2.33   Fig. 2.34   Fig. 2.35

6 Next, introduce some of the filler flowers, which are an important feature. Placed low down, they reinforce the focal area, help to create recession and provide a cushion to assist in positioning the flowers (*Fig. 2.32*).

7 Then, take a group of moluccella or similar material and place them diagonally through the design, remembering to spiral the stems. Fill in where necessary with foliage (*Fig. 2.33*).

8 Add the choice flowers, working them through the design in a group, down to the focal area (*Fig. 2.34*).

9 Introduce a trailing foliage to cascade from the bouquet. It will give movement to the design (*Fig. 2.34*).

10 Add large leaves low down in the design to give it width and so add visual weight to the base (*Fig. 2.35*).

11 To tie the bouquet, take enough raffia or tape to go round the stems several times. Double it into two equal lengths and pass it round the bouquet at the tying point. Thread the two ends through the loop which has been formed and pull it tight. Separate them and pass round the tying point in opposite directions. Finish with a double knot.

12 Trim the ends of the stems to a length approximately one third of the finished bouquet, or to a size appropriate to the vase.

Gift wrapping a front facing tied bouquet

When gift wrapping this bouquet, take care not to crush the flowers at the base of the design. This applies particularly with modern designs, where the foliage and flowers at the base are much wider than with the more traditional styles. Gathering the cellofilm round the tying point is essential to give the bouquet the required fullness.

MATERIALS

Cellofilm
Ribbon
Greetings card, care card
Flower food

METHOD

1 Start with a clean, dry work surface.

2 Cut a piece of cellofilm equal to the length of the bouquet plus 6" (150 mm) (*Fig. 2.36*).

3 Place the sheet of cellofilm on the work surface with the printed side downwards. Position the bouquet on the

6" (150mm)

Fig. 2.36

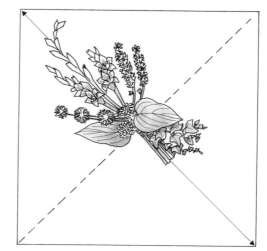

Fig. 2.37   Ensure tie point is in line with corners

Fig. 2.38   Fold both corners over to tying point

cellofilm diagonally, with the tip of the bouquet towards the top left hand corner (*Fig. 2.37*).

4 Fold in the bottom left hand corner and the top right hand corner to the tying point (*Fig. 2.38*).

5 Gather the cellofilm round the tying point to gain the desired fullness at the base.

6 Fix a ribbon bow of a suitable size and colour over the tying point and fasten securely (*Fig. 2.39*).

7 Decorate the bouquet or trim with ribbons etc. as required.

8 The bouquet can be placed in water to await delivery.

Fig. 2.39   Gather to tying point and attach bow securely. Remove surplus Cellocoup

THE PRINCIPLES OF WIRING TECHNIQUES

Because the florist uses materials of such varying size, weight and texture there can be no single method of mounting and wiring them. There are, however, a few basic rules or principles to follow to achieve an acceptable standard of technique and workmanship.

Wiring in floristy can be divided into two categories, depending upon whether the wire is to support or position the materials on which it is to be used.

*S*upporting (Wiring)

A flower, florette or other plant material can be supported either on its own natural stem, or removed and supported on a false stem which the florist creates. In some cases the natural stem may be strong enough to support the material without additional support but where such support is required, the wire used must be as light as is practical and concealed wherever possible.

Flowers must never appear rigid and deprived of the natural rhythm which is the hallmark of the professional florist's work.

*P*ositioning (Mounting)

This is the term given to fixing supported material into the required foundation, base or anchorage. In some cases the same wire can be used to fulfil both functions, supporting and positioning. In such cases, however, the wire used must be heavy enough to ensure secure fixing but not so heavy that it looks clumsy.

*T*o wire or not to wire

Wire should only be used if it is necessary for the support and control of the material being used, and then it should only be of sufficient strength to do the job effectively and no more. Wherever possible the supporting wires should be concealed by wiring the subject internally. There are, however, instances where complete internal wiring is not possible, notably in the case of roses and carnations.

The rose is a comparatively heavy flower with a hard, woody stem, except for a few inches below the calyx where the stem is rigid and brittle. If this part of the stem is supported the flow of moisture through tiny ducts to the bloom is not interrupted and losses due to transpiration are more easily replaced from the water in the container in which the rose has been arranged. A 24 gauge (0.56 mm) wire will give sufficient support to prevent the bloom from bending over.

Carnations also have comparatively hard stems but with brittle joints spaced at regular intervals along its length. The joint immediately below the calix is particularly vulnerable. A 22 gauge (0.71 mm) wire will give sufficient support, but it should be given a complete encircling twist just below the calyx to prevent the bloom being knocked off at this vulnerable joint.

It is of the utmost importance in floristry that wiring is only used where it is absolutely necessary.

The professional florist should know how long a flower or piece of foliage will live in any particular circumstance. If it will remain crisp and fresh if unsupported on its own stem for the required length of time, no wiring is necessary other than for the necessary control to produce a required effect in a design.

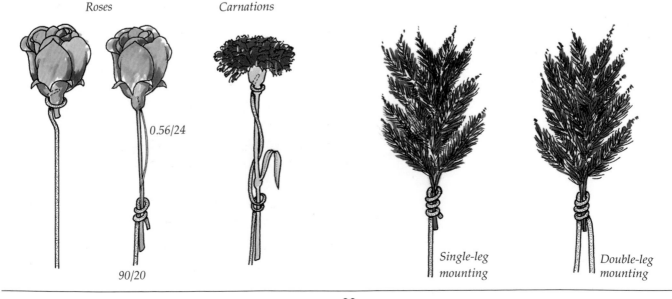

Roses *Carnations*

0.56/24

90/20

Single-leg mounting *Double-leg mounting*

METRICATION OF FLORIST WIRE

UNIT OF WEIGHT

Price £x per 25 kg

SIZES	Recommended sizes	Replacing
	1·25 mm	18 swg
	1·00 mm	19 swg
	0·90 mm	20 swg
	0·71 mm	22 swg
	0·56 mm	24 swg
	0·46 mm	26 swg
	0·38 mm	28 swg
	0·32 mm	30 swg
	0·28 mm	32 swg
	0·24 mm	34 swg
	0·20 mm	36 swg

LENGTHS	Recommended lengths	Replacing
	90 mm	3½ ins
	100 mm	4 ins
	130 mm	5 ins
	150 mm	6 ins
	180 mm	7 ins
	200 mm	8 ins
	230 mm	9 ins
	260 mm	10 ins
	310 mm	12 ins
	360 mm	14 ins
	380 mm	15 ins
	460 mm	18 ins

BUNDLES

Weight per bundle = 2½ kg

REELS

125 grams per reel
10 reels per box
20 boxes per 25 kg pack

Table 1

Buttonholes and corsages

Promoting the sale of flowers for personal adornment can become a good extra sales item and to the enterprising florist it is an excellent way of using up perfect heads from broken or short stemmed blooms, which can be gathered up, recut, and left drinking in bowls beside the work bench.

At first, floristry students may find making corsages time consuming, but with perseverance and learning a few short cuts, particularly with the glue gun, they should soon find this 'floristry in miniature' work most rewarding.

The traditional gentleman's formal buttonhole usually comprises a white flower for formal evening dress and formal morning wear, at a wedding for example, and a crimson flower for wear with a dinner jacket and formal day wear such as a lounge suit.

Ladies may wear a corsage on almost any part of the body including: shoulder, neckline, waist, hip, wrist and ankle.

Before buttonhole and corsage work is commenced, all the materials in use must be protected. Cover the clean and tidy work area with tissue paper or, ideally, fine polythene sheet so that uncompleted work can be covered if the florist is called away unexpectedly.

Gentleman's rose buttonhole

MATERIALS

1 medium size rose
1 large and 6 small rose leaves

METHOD

1. Cut the rose obliquely, leaving a half inch of stem.

2. Place the rose and the leaves in a bowl of water to 'firm up'.

3. Make 3–5 fine hairpins with silver wire and insert them downwards into the calyx. Make sure they go into the seed box. This prevents the rose from 'blowing' (*Fig. 3.1*).

4. Insert a 22 gauge (0.71 mm) wire up the stem and take silver wire through and down to prevent 'spinning'. Tape wires (*Fig. 3.1*).

5. Wire the rose leaves on silver wires, using the single leg stitching method as shown and tape them (*Fig. 3.2*).

6. Place one large leaf centrally and one on each side.

7. Add the rose to the leaves.

THE PRINCIPLES OF WIRING TECHNIQUES 3

Fig. 3.1   Angle hairpin down into seed box to prevent 'blowing'. Take silver wire down and tape to stem wire

Fig. 3.2   Place two leaves together back to back and position behind the rose

Fig. 3.3   Bend single front leaf down. Don't forget a pin

8 Finish the front of the buttonhole with one leaf which has been turned back and three at the back for protection (*Fig. 3.3*).

9 Wire the buttonhole together firmly and tape.

10 Gently turn the rose slightly forward.

11 Spray with a fine mister and add a 1" (25 mm) pin before delivery.

See Plate 8

Carnation buttonhole
——————————— MATERIALS ———————————
One carnation
Suitable foliage eg.: carnation grass, spiky house plant foliage or safari foliage

METHOD

1 Cut the carnation obliquely, ½" (12 mm) below the head.

2 Insert a 22 gauge (0.71 mm) wire up into the carnation. Insert a silver wire through the base of the head and down to prevent 'spinning'.

3 Conceal all the mechanics with tape.

4 Wire and tape the required amount of foliage.

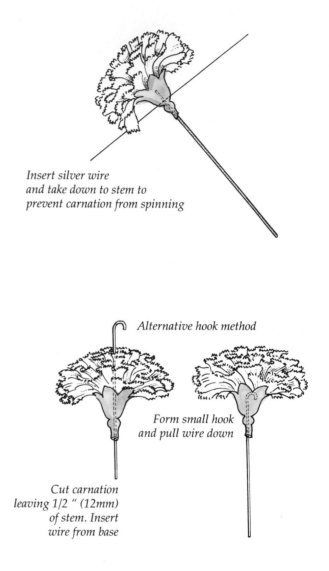

Insert silver wire and take down to stem to prevent carnation from spinning

Alternative hook method

Form small hook and pull wire down

Cut carnation leaving 1/2 " (12mm) of stem. Insert wire from base

5 Turn the carnation slightly forward and position the foliage to form a pleasing design.

6 Bind with silver reel wire and tape to finish.

7 Spray with fine mister.

8 Insert a 1" (25 mm) pin before delivery.

See Plate 9

Orchid corsage

One orchid
Decorative foliage eg.: dracaena, asparagus, meyeri, pteris, hedera, dizygotheca etc.

METHOD

1 Cut the orchid diagonally from its stem, about ½″ (12 mm) below the head.

2 Insert a 22 gauge (0.71 mm) wire up into the orchid head.

3 Tape a silver wire for half its length.

4 Thread the bare end of the wire through the base of the front of the 'throat' of the orchid. Tape the remaining length of wire.

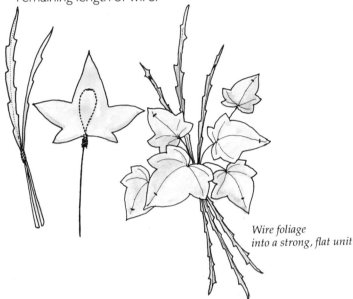

*Wire foliage
into a strong, flat unit*

5 Bring down both ends of the silver wire and tape them to the 22 gauge stub wire so that no untaped silver wire is showing at the base of the orchid.

6 Wire and tape all the foliage to be used.

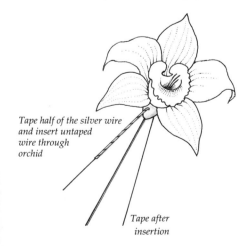

*Tape half of the silver wire
and insert untaped
wire through
orchid*

*Tape after
insertion*

7 Make a strong, flat back unit of foliage and position the orchid, slightly tilted forward, onto it. Arrange the foliage, in patterns, throughout the design.

8 Tape and finish.

9 Spray with fine mister.

10 Insert pearl-headed pin before delivery.

See Plate 10

The mixed corsage

MATERIALS

Flowers: carol roses, gypsophila paniculata, dendrobium orchids
Foliage: Ficus bejamina variegata, sedum

METHOD

1 Wire and tape all materials using the finest wires to achieve sufficient support and control (*Fig. 3.4*).

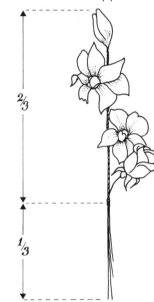

⅔

⅓

Support design on
24 gauge wire and
tape together for
strength above
focal point

Tape and wire all material

Fig. 3.4

THE PRINCIPLES OF WIRING TECHNIQUES 3

Fig. 3.5   Add foliage radiating from the focal point to create the outline

2 Select a bud for the top of the design. For extra support insert a 24 g (0.56 mm) wire from the bottom to give extra support to the back of the design. Neatly tape.

3 Place second flower and gradually continue down the backbone of the design to the tie point which will determine the focal point. As a reference guide, the proportion of two thirds to one third should be adhered to.

Add the focal flower directly above the tie point.

To achieve a good design, all the other materials should be arranged in patterns, to radiate from this point (*Fig. 3.5*).

This is the widest part of the design.

Fig. 3.6   Add side flowers to emphasise focal flower and complete by filling in with foliage

4 Add some taped buds and foliage to the front of the assembly to form a return end, making sure that the tie point remains in one place (*Fig. 3.6*).

5 When the design is completed, the latter placements can be gently pulled back and adjusted to allow the corsage to sit comfortably on the wearer.

6 Spray with fine mister.

7 Before delivery, add one or two corsage pins, depending on the size of finished design.

See Plate 11

*I*ntroduction

In floristry, design determines the way we choose and use our materials: the way every piece of floristry is planned and organised to give the maximum visual appeal.

The elements of design guide us in creating visually attractive work. However, such guidelines are not rigid. They allow freedom and flexibility to express one's own style. It is important to understand the elements of design which are:

- colour
- form
- space
- texture

*C*olour

Whilst line is the basic component of design, colour provides emotion. Countless books have been written on colour, yet few people understand its full emotional impact. A colour that inspires and cheers one person, can irritate another. Colours can be warm or cold, sending out cheerful or soothing vibrations.

Primary colours

Secondary colours

Tertiary colours

Complementary colours

Analogous colours

Monochromatic colours

It is essential for florists to understand the basics of colour and how it can be used. This section will lay the foundations for that understanding, starting with an explanation of the colour wheel. The colour wheel has several colour groups but the three most basic ones are:

*P*rimary colours

Red, blue and yellow – are the sources of all colours. Primary colours cannot be created by mixing colours.

*S*econdary colours

Green, orange and violet – are created when two primary colours that are next to each other on the colour wheel are mixed in equal proportions.

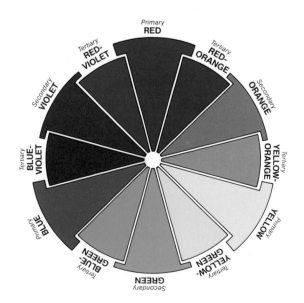

The Colour Wheel

Tertiary colours

Or intermediate colours, are obtained by mixing equal parts of a primary colour and a secondary colour that lies next to it.

Colour has three dimensions: hue, value and chroma:

- Hue is the name of a particular colour, thus 'hue' is not synonymous with 'colour'.
- Chroma is a colour's intensity or saturation.
- Value is a colour's lightness or darkness.

Tints, shades and tones all affect a colour's value:

- Tints are created when white is added to a colour.
- Shades occur when black is added to a colour.
- Tones are colours with grey added.

Light affects colours differently depending upon its intensity. Under reduced lighting, for example, some colours will appear to be almost black, whilst others, like pale lavender will really come to life. Beyond the three basic colour groups there are also additional ones.

Complementary colours

Complementary colours are colours opposite each other on the colour wheel, like blue and orange, violet and yellow, red and green. They are warm and cool colours. The complementary colour harmony is the brightest colour harmony there is because its colours are opposing. They give you the greatest contrast. Contrast can also be heightened by the intensity of the colours you choose.

Designing with complementary colours creates greater impact with fewer flowers. Complementary arrangements look wonderful in large rooms like banquet halls or lobbies but tend to overpower smaller areas.

Colours are also frequently described as advancing or receding. Advancing colours are warm colours like reds, yellows, oranges, red-violet and yellow-green. Receding colours are cool hues like blues, greens, blue-violet and violets.

Many florists think the most important thing about colour and design is knowing the receding and advancing colours and how they affect people. You should know how people are emotionally affected by colour. Warm (advancing) colours and cool (receding) colours have an automatic emotional impact. People generally have a preference for either warm or cool colours. Preference also depends on mood and what

people need. You can choose warm colours if you want to cheer people up or cool colours if you want a formal or soothing feeling.

Analogous colours

Analogous colours are made up of adjoining colours consisting of one primary, one secondary and two tertiary colours.

When you choose analogous colours, it is best to pick those that fall either on the cool side of the harmony or the warm side, because an analogous harmony generally has an emotional feel to it. The easiest way to remember analogous harmonies is to think of the harmonies of nature, like the red-violets and violets in a sunset. Or think of autumn with its yellows, oranges and browns or the harmony of forest greens, blue lakes and the blue sky.

Adjacent colours reinforce each other and create a close harmony. When these colours are used in groups, they create analogous colour schemes.

Monochromatic colours

A monochromatic colour scheme is one colour and its full range of tints, shades and tones. For example, sky blue to medium blue to navy blue and all shades and tints in between is a monochromatic colour scheme. When used in a floral arrangement, this scheme has a retreating, subdued character.

Colour summary

To sum up, here is a list of some of the important elements of colour.

- *Primary colours:* Red, blue and yellow.
- *Secondary colours:* Orange, green and violet. Created by mixing two primary colours.
- *Tertiary colours:* Red-orange, blue-violet, red-violet, blue-green, yellow-orange and yellow-green, created by mixing a primary colour with either secondary colour located next to it on the colour wheel.
- *Warm colours:* Reds, red-violet, oranges, yellows and yellow-green. These are also called *advancing* colours.
- *Cool colours:* Blues, greens, blue-violet and violet. Also known as *receding* colours.
- *Neutral colours:* White, black and grey.

- *Tones:* A variation or a graduation of a colour, achieved by adding grey.
- *Chroma:* A colour's intensity; its brightness or dullness.
- *Value:* A colour's lightness or darkness. Affected by tints, tones or shades.
- *Complementary colours:* Colours opposite each other on the colour wheel.
- *Analogous colours:* One primary, one secondary colour and two adjacent tertiary colours on the colour wheel.
- *Triad:* A combination of any three colours equally distant from one another on the colour wheel.
- *Polychromatic colours:* A combination of five or more colours on the colour wheel.
- *Monochromatic colours:* A range of tints and shades based on a single colour.

Round materials attract the eye and are generally used for focal flowers. Round shapes, used at the base of a design, stabilise it. Gerberas, roses and carnations, are several examples.

Transitional materials are used as stepping stones to link round and line materials together. Spray carnations and spray chrysanthemums are often used for this purpose.

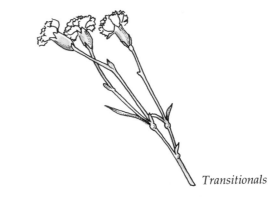

Transitionals

*F*orm

Use a variety of shapes within a design as the contrast between them provides interest. Line material is generally used to give height and break up solid, round shapes. Their spikey shapes give movement to a design: gladioli, larkspur and bullrushes are typical examples.

*S*pace

The use of maximum space within a design will both define and enhance the material being used. Designs with flowers tightly packed together, allowing no space between them, will result in a solid, static appearance.

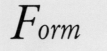

Lines   *Rounds*

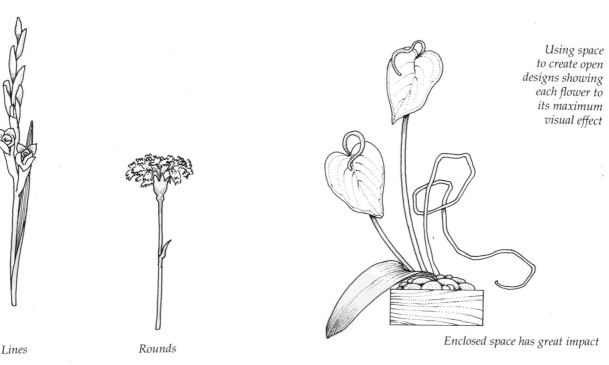

Using space to create open designs showing each flower to its maximum visual effect

Enclosed space has great impact

Plate 6   Twelve red roses, hand tied

Plate 6a   Hand tied bouquet

Plate 7   Front facing, hand tied arrangement

Plate 8
Gentleman's rose
buttonhole

Plate 11
Mixed corsage

Plate 9
Carnation buttonhole

Plate 10
Orchid corsage

4

DESIGN IN FLORISTRY

Texture

Visual textures, in any good design, should be varied. This is particularly important when creating a design which is all in one colour. For example, an all-white arrangement could look bland without the added interest given by differing textures.

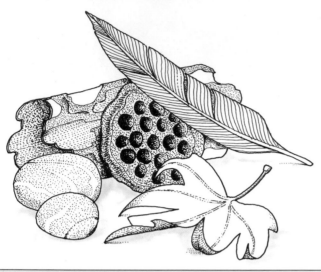

The principles of design

To create visually attractive floristry it is important to understand the following principles of design:

- Balance
- Proportion
- Rhythm
- Contrast
- Dominance
- Harmony

Balance

There are two types of balance: actual and visual. In design we are concerned with visual balance. An arrangement can look unbalanced without actually falling over. To achieve good visual balance, the materials must be used and positioned with care. It is not always necessary to use two items of equal size to achieve visual balance. A single, large flower can be balanced by a group of smaller ones. A large, shiny leaf, used low down in a design, looks visually heavy and can balance a group of very tall flowers.

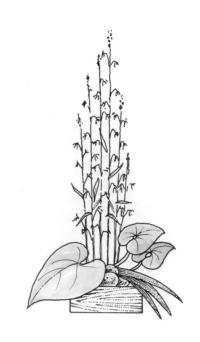

Proportion

To achieve good proportions consideration must be given to many interdependent factors

Sizes graded for a harmonious effect

Proportion is the relationship of the parts of the design, the arrangement to its container and the whole composition to its setting. Good proportion is dependent on many things:

- The visual weight of the chosen flowers and foliage. An example of poor proportion would be very large flowers in a small container.
- The visual weight of the container.
- The setting of the design. The style and size of the design and its container will be determined by its location.

All three factors will determine the height and width of the finished design. There are no absolute rules on proportion.

Scale

Scale concerns the sizes of the individual items within the design. Too great a difference in size between the flowers will lead to an uncomfortable looking design. For example, a large chrysanthemum bloom and a small freesia are two extremes of size. Transitional material, such as spray chrysanthemums may be required to link the two together. To produce a harmonious design, grading the sizes of the materials within the arrangement is essential.

Rhythm

Rhythm is an expression of movement, a necessary component in a design to draw the eye from one part of the design to the next. A design which lacks rhythm is static and boring. There are many ways of creating rhythmic appeal:

- Grouping flowers through the design gives a sense of movement and continuity.

- Curved lines create greater movement than straight ones.

- Recession, achieved by placing some flowers at lower levels than others, is also important.

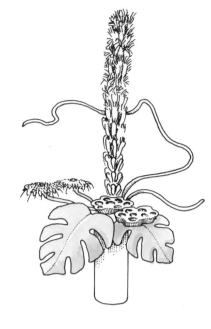

Careful choice of flowers and variety of shapes, textures and colours create an interesting design

Contrast

Contrast is achieved by using a variety of colours, shapes and textures, which are all important elements in a design if monotony is to be avoided. Carefully planning and using the Elements of Design will give the variety necessary in a perfect design.

Dominance

Dominance in a design lies in emphasising one, or more, areas of the design above the others. Generally in floristry, dominant areas are called *focal points*. There can be more than one focal point in a design.

Large, round shapes, bold colours and shiny textures can be used to create areas of greater dominance within a design.

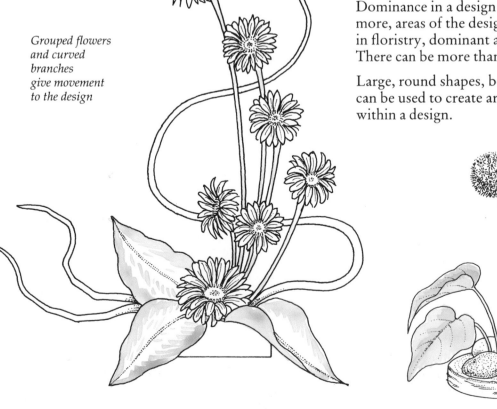

Grouped flowers and curved branches give movement to the design

Large round shapes, with shiny textures, create the design's area of dominance

DESIGN IN FLORISTRY

4

Harmony

When a combination of all the Principles and Elements of design have been well used, harmony will result. It is the final achievement and there will be total agreement between all parts of the design.

The key to creative floristry is a well thought out design plan.

Plate 12   Arrangement showing the impact of unusual foliage

Plate 13   Symmetrical arrangement

Plate 14 Country style basket arrangement

*I*ntroduction

Skilfully designed flower arrangements are a form of art which are enjoyed not only by the designers who create them, but more widely by everyone who sees them. Since they form a large part of our gift business, a high standard of design and presentation is essential.

A well chosen selection of foliage and plant materials, skilfully arranged to complement or contrast with their surroundings, will enhance any occasion whether it be held at home or in a public building.

Our customers send flower arrangements to express happiness, sympathy, or maybe just to share with a friend the sheer beauty of the materials used.

Because there are so many different styles and designs of arrangement, it is important that the florist is aware of the occasion for which the arrangement is required and the surroundings in which it will be seen, so that the most suitable colours and design can be recommended to the customer.

To plan an arrangement successfully it is essential that the principles of design are fully understood. The section on design in this manual should be carefully studied.

There are many points to bear in mind before constructing an arrangement. First among them are:

- The *scale* and *proportion* of the finished arrangement to its surroundings.

- The container should be clean and checked to ensure that it is watertight. Is the container suitable for the occasion? Will it hold sufficient foam to support the materials being used?

- The foam must be cut to the correct size. Remember that sufficient space must be left between the foam and the container to allow the design to be watered easily. The container should always be kept filled with water. Thoroughly soak the foam and securely fix it to the container. Foam which is inadequately soaked will draw moisture down the flower stems and cause them to dehydrate.

- The materials chosen should be fresh and well conditioned if they are to give lasting pleasure to the recipient.

- Flower stems should be clean of the lower foliage and cut to an oblique point so that they can be pushed well into the foam and securely held without causing the foam to crumble or break.

Wherever possible, the stems should reach the water level in the container so that they can take up the maximum amount of moisture.

- The correct placement of flowers and foliage in the design will give it stability. The colour placements should provide visual balance.

- When completed, the design should have a clearly defined shape and outline with all the foam concealed and the back of the arrangement tidily finished with short pieces of foliage.

- If the arrangement is for delivery, it is essential that the card and its envelope are neatly written and correctly spelt, it is also advisable to include instructions for watering.

An arrangement, beautifully presented, will give lasting pleasure.

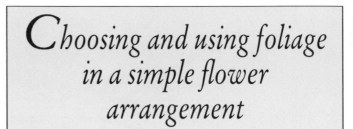

*C*hoosing and using foliage in a simple flower arrangement

Flower shops stock many types of decorative foliage and customers expect to find them in their gift designs.

There is a wide choice for the florist who learns the beauty of the length and curve of the stem, the different structures and shapes of leaves and the haunting, soft colourings of bark and foliage. (**See Plate 12.**)

Expensive, choice foliage does not automatically make a flower arrangement good. Two pieces of cupressus, seen with an imaginative eye, can create a lovely effect. It is using foliage in a discriminating way that triumphs.

Even a modest flower arrangement needs a careful choice of two varieties of foliage with different growth and structure and between three and five large, single leaves. With the arrangement in mind, flowers and foliage should be chosen together, complementing each other and in correct proportion.

Find the elegant, vertical foliage stem to establish height. Look for the spike and slender growth that will outline shape. See the variety of leaf shapes and sizes. Understand the beauty of stems. Seek subtle colourings where stems and leaves echo flower shades, creating excitement and a transition of colour.

Note sleek and rough textures.

When making a simple, one-sided arrangement make the first placement a strong vertical, using a slim, structured piece of foliage. Then trace the arrangement's outline shape with slender tips. Actual and visual balance has begun.

The foliage must be grouped or lined through the design, not dotted around haphazardly. For strength and clarity, run one variety of foliage through one variety of flower. Use it at varying heights and placements to create depth and interest. Recess the big, dark, single leaves to emphasise the focal area.

In the case of flowers with a robust foliage – lilies, iris, gladioli and daffodils for example, the flowers' own foliage can be used. Otherwise, choose a foliage of similar colour and character. When a flower has insignificant foliage, the carnation, for example, variegation can be introduced effectively.

On occasions, two or three stems of the same foliage can be used together as a group. Its colouring and different growth structure will contrast with the flower heads surrounding it.

The continental style of flower design is full of beautifully textured foliage: moss, seedheads and fruits, bedded down onto the foam. These are contoured and grouped together to emphasise their individual beauty. We can adapt this grouping idea to enrich our own conventional work.

It has been said of foam flower arrangement work, 'Put your foliage in first. It is quicker and covers the foam'. But unless it is followed by the statement, 'The rules of design always apply', it is unwise and can be misleading. Even if you are only seeking to cover the foam, design rules must be foremost in your mind.

Separate the foliage by colour, form and shape. Use it properly; tips to the outside with the heavier leaves holding the centre together.

Merely covering the foam with odd bits of foliage leads to design faults in visual weight, grouping and line that can never be overcome. Trying to correct them makes holes all over the foam, particularly around the focal area. This is not good craftsmanship.

Building foliage into a flower arrangement involves a high level of skill. The foliage is beautifully shown in its own right as an element of the design and the foam is fairly well covered. All that is then needed are a few matching pieces of foliage here and there.

An expensive, bigger flower arrangement needs stricter and more discerning control of foliage varieties. In your anxiety do not create a wild hedge. Hold fast to the simple and strong concepts of good design and produce a calm, peaceful arrangement of great beauty that will be a joy to receive.

Plate 15
Country basket

Plate 15a
Standard basket

Plate 15b Shallow basket

Plate 15c Modern basket

Plate 15d Golden basket

Plate 15e Dainty basket

Vertical line arrangement

This form of line arrangement can be a very beautiful, simple style, showing to advantage the texture and colour of the plant material. Vertical line arrangements are usually designed with a limited number of flowers of one variety. Bold, strong flower shapes are particularly lovely, and great care must be taken when placing them as each flower must be positioned correctly to achieve the correct balance.

Large leaves at the base of the arrangement will give emphasis to the flowers and add solidity and balance to the finished design.

A shallow ceramic container or dish is most suitable for this type of design.

Rhythm can be created within the arrangement with the use of a curving branch which will draw the eye through the arrangement.

MATERIALS

Ceramic dish
Small piece of foam
Suitable flowers: five carnations, roses, gerbera or anthuriums, strelitzia etc.
Suitable foliage: five large leaves. eg. dieffenbachia, croton, hosta etc.

SUNDRIES

Bun moss, pebbles, slate, contorted willow, larch etc.

METHOD

1 A small plastic frog is glued to the dish first and the foam firmly pushed onto it for security (*Fig. 5.1*).

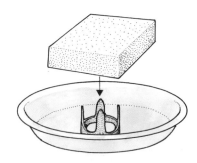

Fig. 5.1

2 Make sure the foam is thoroughly soaked.

3 Place first flower towards far side of foam to give space for other insertions of plant material.

4 Insert the next flower, cut a little shorter, and placed in front of and to one side of the first flower (*Fig. 5.2*).

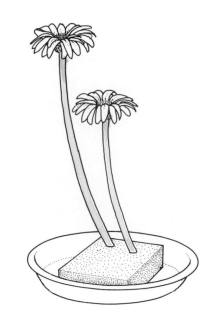

Fig. 5.2

5 Continue placing flowers in this vertical pattern, shortening the length of stem, and using the most open flower for the last placement at the base of the design. This will be the focal flower (*Fig. 5.3*).

Fig. 5.3

6 The contorted willow or larch added at this stage will create movement and rhythm.

7 To give width and substance to the base of the design, carefully position the large leaves to surround the focal flower.

8 Finish with bun moss pinned to the foam, or, use pebbles, slate etc. to conceal the mechanics and add interest to the base of the arrangement.

Posy arrangement

A posy arrangement is a circular design which may be seen from every angle. Although posy arrangements can be made to any size, they are generally regarded as a small low design, suitable to place on a coffee table or dining table.

Dainty flowers and foliage give a far more open look to this design than will large round flowers. Recession at the centre and space between the flowers are most important to create a three dimensional effect, otherwise the arrangement will look heavy and static.

Choose flowers and foliage which are in proportion to one another. Study their *size* and *shape*. Decide how big the posy can be to make the most of the chosen materials.

Choice flowers such as freesia, roses etc. should be placed high in the design in a prominent position. They can be grouped together in the centre or placed diagonally through the design. Make every flower work within the design, showing each one to its full beauty and value.

Do not be tempted to complicate the design. Discipline your mind not to overcrowd the arrangement.

MATERIALS

A low flat dish
Suitable foliage: eucalyptus, leather leaf, myrtle, pittosporum, ivy, rosettes of foliage
Suitable flowers: freesia, roses, spray carnations, nerines
Transitional flowers: alchemilla mollis, sweet peas, monte casino, gypsophila, statice, achillea.

METHOD

1 Using a saucer-like container, fit a round of foam and secure it with tape of a matching or blending colour, leaving ample space for watering (*Fig. 5.4*).

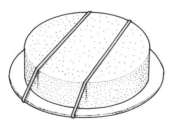

Fig. 5.4   Tape foam to container

2 To create the initial round outline, take five pieces of light foliage, eg. eucalyptus, all of the same size and firmly push them into the foam at equal distances from one another. The foliage should rest on the lip of the container angled downwards so that it lightly touches the work surface (*Fig. 5.5*).

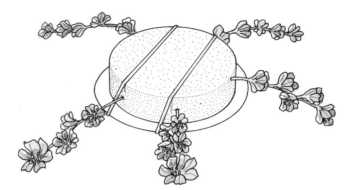

Fig. 5.5   First placements of foliage all the same size and placed at equal distances around base to achieve outline

3 Group a second, different variety of foliage between the first five placements of the circle to strengthen the outline. More of the same foliage is stepped towards the centre to create an elevated profile and conceal the mechanics (*Fig. 5.6*).

4 As you progess, keep turning the arrangement so that all areas are worked evenly to create a balanced design. *All materials should appear to radiate from the focal area* (*Fig. 5.7*).

5 Group your choice flowers in the centre of the foam, starting with one flower that has a long straight stem. Remembering that this will be your most prominent flower, carefully cut it to height. A first placement which is too short will produce a flat, squat design.

Fig. 5.6   Second placement of foliage

Plate 16   All round arrangement

Fig. 5.7 First choice flowers grouped in centre of foam, reducing in height to create shape

Fig. 5.8 Conceal foam with larger foliage and start grouping second choice flowers

6 Arrange the remaining choice flowers around this first placement, lowering each one to produce a group at differing heights. Large leaves should now be added to the base of the arrangement to give depth and accentuate the focal flowers (*Fig. 5.8*).

7 Using your grouped foliage as a guide, step groups of flowers into the design at equal distances. Use buds and dainty flowers for the lateral placements, place them low into the sides of the foam, within the encircling ring of foliage, recessing some and extending others to the profile. Check the design to see that all the mechanics are covered. Aim for a professional finish.

Symmetrical arrangement

The symmetrical arrangement is a traditional design which can be made to any size, and can range from a locker in a hospital ward to a pedestal in a church. The symmetrical arrangement is usually placed against a wall and although it is mainly viewed from the front, the sides are also seen so the profile is equally important to the design.

This type of arrangement can be made from a variety of materials, but the best effect is usually achieved by using flowers of differing shapes and sizes which can be grouped for added interest and impact. Colour has immediate customer appeal and must be skilfully chosen and blended.

Choose flowers and foliage carefully to achieve good proportion and scale. A large, symmetrical pedestal arrangement will obviously need bigger, bolder flowers than a locker arrangement where dainty materials are called for.

Foliage plays an important role by enhancing the flowers. Use a variety of foliage for interest.

The choice of flowers and foliage is the most important decision you will make. Learn how to select them.

- Tall, elegant flowers like liatris.
- Bold shapes such as roses or carnations.
- Transitional shapes like spray carnations or spray chrysanthemums.

All these different shapes are needed to create a lovely design.

The finished arrangement should have immediate impact, provoking a pleasing, positive effect on the recipient.

MATERIALS

Suitable container: low dish or pedestal vase
Suitable foliage: pittosporum, eucalyptus, ruscus, nephrolepsis, cyclamen leaves, ivy
Suitable flowers: most flowers are suitable, for example: liatris, carnations, roses, freesia, spray chrysanthemums, dendrobium orchids, larkspur, gerbera.

FLOWER ARRANGEMENTS 5

PREPARATION

The amount of foam used depends on the quantity of flowers. Never be mean with it; using an inadequate amount of foam will lead to disintegration and the foam will dry out prematurely. When judging the quantity of foam needed, make sure there will be enough room left in the container to add water without spillage.

Cut the foam to the size required and make sure it is adequately soaked through the centre. Foam which is thoroughly soaked will almost submerge in a bowl of water. If it is still dry inside, it will bob about on the surface. Secure the foam firmly to the container with pot tape.

METHOD

1 Select flowers and foliage, checking the order for special flowers or a chosen colour harmony. If nothing is specified, select the flowers for their colour harmony, but not forgetting the importance of shape and texture. Perfume may also be a consideration.

2 Foliage should be chosen for its shape and texture. For example, eucalyptus, pussy willow and cyclamen leaves would complement each other.

3 Start by determining the outline shape of the arrangement. Select a tall, slender piece of foliage, cut the end to an oblique point and remove any leaves and side shoots from the lower three or four inches of its length.

4 Insert it approximately one third in from the back of the foam. The position of this first placement is important as sufficient room must be left for subsequent placements and provide balance and depth to the design. All material should be inserted sufficiently into the foam to hold securely.

5 Cut two suitable pieces of choice foliage for lateral placements, each of them should be about half the length of the first, vertical placement. Cut them and clean the lower stems. Insert them on either side of the foam, in line with the base of the vertical stem, low in the foam and flowing over the sides of the container to create a triangular shape (Fig. 5.9).

6 These three placements establish the height and width of the arrangement.

A further forward placement of the same length as the laterals and flowing over the front of the container will establish the depth.

7 Strengthen the outline and depth with patterns of foliage inserted between the verticals and laterals. Start to introduce larger and darker leaves at the base of the design to add visual strength to the design. Do not cover all the surface area of the foam at this stage (Fig. 5.10).

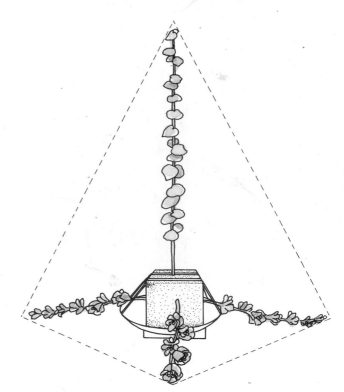

Fig. 5.9   First four foliage placements determine outline shape

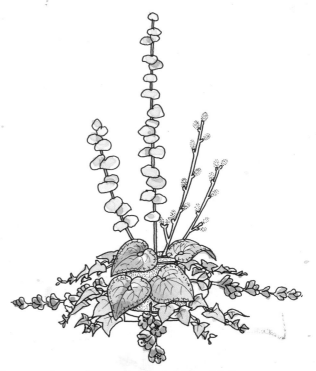

Fig. 5.10   Strengthen outline with grouped foliage

8 Flowers can be grouped for either shape or colour. Grouping will add interest and give impact to the design, but care should be taken to ensure that the visual balance of the arrangement is maintained. The first flower placement should be chosen carefully to create the required height. Use a small bud or pointed flower.

Fig. 5.11 Profile of arrangement showing placement of choice flowers

Fig. 5.12 Foliage removed to emphasise flower placement

9 Small flowers are used for the lateral placements. The stems are cut to approximately half the length of the vertical flower and inserted into each side of the foam, flowing over the sides of the container and within the framework of the foliage. This will give the width of the arrangement and complete the triangular shape.

10 Choice flowers are then worked through the centre of the design, reducing in stem length towards the focal area and extending outwards over the edge of the container to establish the depth.

11 A flower placed behind the first vertical will give greater depth to the arrangement. Add to the depth by placing flowers and foliage behind the vertical (*Fig. 5.11*).

12 Transitional flowers, recessed and elevated, moving through the arrangement, complete the outline and profile.

Good use of space between the flowers will allow them to breathe and open. It will also make the arrangement look lighter and larger.

Larger headed flowers or darker materials recessed below the choice, centre flowers will emphasise and enhance their importance.

13 To complete the arrangement, any visible foam must be covered. Extra care should be given to the foam at the back so that the design is well finished (*Fig. 5.12*).

14 Add shorter foliage at both the back and sides keeping it well within the shape of the finished arrangement until the foam is concealed. Leave a space at the back of the design so that it can be easily watered.

15 Add more water to the container to make sure that all the material is drinking and finish by spraying with a fine mist sprayer.

See Plate 13

*B*asket arrangement

Basketware and flowers are both natural materials which are sympathetic and go together well. Its form and texture make the basket arrangement an appealing gift for most occasions. **(See Plate 14).**

Baskets are available in a variety of shapes and sizes. Those most often used in commercial floristry have a hooped handle. They are usually round or oval and shallow with a water tight insert or container.

MATERIALS

A suitable basket
One third of a block of soaked foam
Adhesive florist tape or Polytie
Foam fix

FLOWER ARRANGEMENTS

5

Suitable foliage:
For height: eucalyptus, pittosporum, euonymus
For design: sword fern, leather leaf, ruscus
For focal point: hosta, large ivy, alchemilla
Suitable flowers:
For value: roses, carnations, gerbera, freesia
For shape, outline and emphasis: spray carnations, dendrobiums, spray roses
For recession and reinforcement: single ayr, pinks, spray carnations.

Basket preparation

Position the watertight container in the basket. Cover the base of a frog with foam fix and stick it to the container centrally, beneath the basket handle.

Trim the foam so that it will extend 2″ above the sides of the basket and be big enough to hold all the flowers securely. Place the foam on the frog slightly off-centre. Secure the foam to the basket by stretching a length of Polytie across each side of the handle. (A small piece of stem on the top edges of the foam will prevent the tie cutting into it.) (*Fig. 5.13*).

A few small pieces of foliage radiating from the centre of the foam will break up its outline and mask the mechanics.

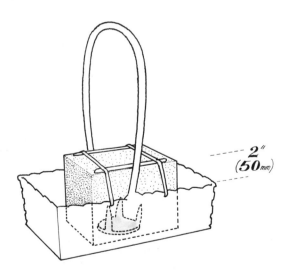

Fig. 5.13 Fix foam just off centre

Assembling the arrangement

The arrangement is determined by the shape of the basket. It must be carefully proportioned so not to obscure or submerge the basket. Flowers may extend above the handle but they must not hide it or get in the way when the basket is lifted or carried.

The completed arrangement should look attractive from any angle. It must be well balanced with a clear focal point of choice flowers from which other materials extend. Carefully grouping the colours and flowers gives the design distinction.

The basket may be seen to better effect if the arrangement is made diagonally across it.

METHOD

1 Begin with a flower placed vertically. Cut the stem obliquely and insert it about 1½″ (40 mm) into the centre of the foam beside the handle. The height of this placement will determine the overall size of the arrangement. Two more flowers of differing heights are placed either side of the first placement and angled slightly.
Light stems of upright foliage are inserted between the flower placements (*Fig. 5.14*).

2 Establish the width of the design with the same type of flowers placed through the arrangement at varying levels.

3 Working at a slight diagonal across the basket, place stems of smaller flowers horizontally into the ends of the foam to establish the length of the design (*Fig. 5.15*).

4 Begin to introduce foliage, keeping it well within the outline of flowers. Larger leaves low down in the foam radiate from beneath the focal point to reinforce it (*Fig. 5.16*).

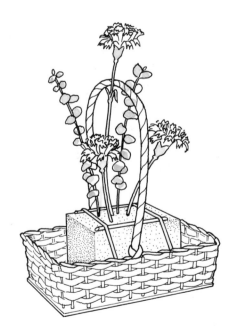

Fig. 5.14 The first flower placement should be central, and the second and third placements should fall either side of the first

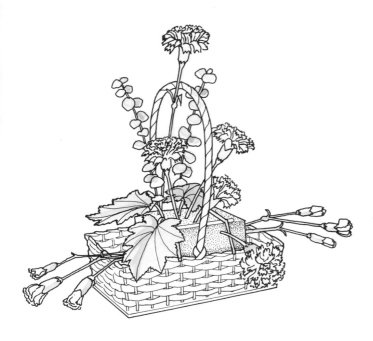

Fig. 5.15 Create outline by adding carnation sprays either end. Ensure three large foliage leaves radiate from focal point

Fig. 5.16

5 Develop the focal point with choice flowers. A grouping of delicate flowers such as dendrobiums added at this point can give the design distinction and impact.

6 Build up the outline with buds and small flowers. Recess flowers to conceal any obvious mechanics.

See Plates 15, 15a, 15b, 15c, 15d and 15e

*A*ll round arrangement

This style of arrangement is a beautiful, natural, flowing design which is best displayed on a circular table in a large hall, the top of the font in a church or, perhaps, on a pedestal in a display area in a showroom.

A clearly thought out plan is essential before attempting this arrangement. The florist has the opportunity to place groups of different choice flowers through the design, skilfully blend their colours, or work them in blocks of colour to make the design more distinctive.

To help you to choose your materials effectively make a simple outline sketch before starting.

An all round arrangement uses the same principles of construction as a simple posy, but the size and variety of the materials needed, demands greater design skill.

MATERIALS

Suitable flowers and foliage: the design described here uses three groups of choice flowers plus transitional materials. The key element is visual balance to which each group must contribute.
Choice flowers: lilies, carnations, roses, gerbera
Transitional flowers: spray carnations, monte casino, spray chrysanthemums, spray roses, statice
Line foliage: eucalyptus, ruscus, sword fern
Bold design foliage: hosta, ivy, euonymus, ming fern, dieffenbachia
Suitable container: a round container of sufficient strength and depth with adequate space for water.

METHOD

1 Take a generous amount of foam for the quantity of flowers used. Soak it and secure it to the container neatly with pot tape (*Fig. 5.17*).

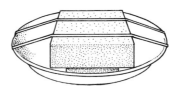

Fig. 5.17

2 Select a slender piece of foliage and place it with care vertically in the very centre of the foam. This placement determines the height of the arrangement

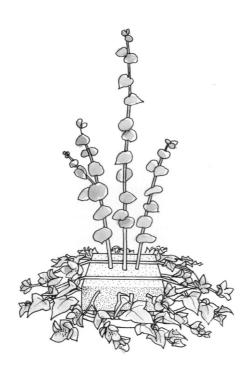

Fig. 5.18 Create width, height and depth by foliage placement and grouping

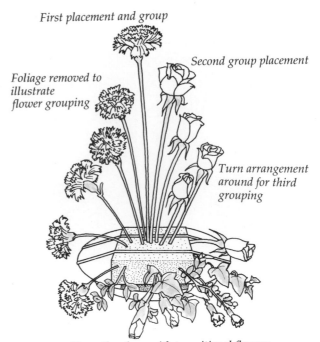

First placement and group

Second group placement

Foliage removed to illustrate flower grouping

Turn arrangement around for third grouping

Strengthen base with transitional flowers

Fig. 5.19

so the length must be carefully chosen. Reinforce it with two or three shorter pieces of the same type of foliage placed around it.

3 Six placements, equally spaced around the foam will create a circular outline and establish the width.

4 Intersperse these placements with other foliage to create a balanced pattern. Use bold foliage in groups, working from the periphery to the centre. This will give depth to the design (*Fig. 5.18*).

5 Select one group of choice flowers. From them, find the one with the most slender and straight stem and place it vertically into the centre of the foam. This will be the tallest flower.

6 Using all the flowers of one type, start with the tallest vertical placement and work progressively downwards and outwards to establish the profile of your design.

7 Taking the second group of flowers, work to one side of the first section. The first flower of this group is placed towards the centre of the foam vertically, but below the tallest flower in the first group. Using the top and sides of the foam, group the flowers so that they appear to radiate from the centre (*Fig. 5.19*).

8 Repeat this pattern in the third section.

9 Having used all the choice flowers, start to strengthen the base of the arrangement by using transitional flowers to flow over the sides of the container and create the width needed to balance the design.

10 Blend the colours and shapes of transitional flowers within the groups, using some open flowers recessed into the centre of the arrangement to give depth and draw the eye into the design. Make sure the foam is adequately covered – one flower head recessed lower into the foam is more effective than just using foliage.

11 Spray lightly with a water mister.

See Plate 16

Introduction

Funeral tributes are the mainstay of commercial floristry. As an expression of sympathy at a time of bereavement a well executed tribute is unsurpassable. However, when customers are selecting a tribute which truly expresses their feelings, your careful guidance and sympathetic attention will be called for.

Prepare yourself before attempting to take a funeral order. Study the Selection Guide/Sympathy Guide. Know what flower stocks are available. Learn about bases and foundations in case an unusual design is requested. For instance a family with naval connections may request an anchor. **(See Plate 17.)** Familiarise yourself with your shop's pricing policy. Be prepared to explain to a customer any floristry terms you may have to use.

A customer who is upset and undecided will need sympathetic but positive persuasion. A florist must be able to concentrate and obtain all the essential information without adding to the customer's distress, and by avoiding mistakes and misunderstandings which can never be satisfactorily rectified.

Fine quality floristry stands out at a funeral and brings credit to your shop. Never undersell. Aim for perfection. Foam bases have revolutionised floristry. When well used they make possible natural, uncontrived designs of great beauty.

Always ensure that foam is firmly fixed to its container, and that stems are securely anchored. Good proportions, a clearly defined shape, and design are important. Well conditioned, mature flowers enhance the value of your work and ensure customer satisfaction. Don't be tempted to use materials which are past their best. One complaint can undo the benefit of much expensive advertising.

Carefully check every tribute. Is it well finished and worthy of your shop? Remember, as well as flowers we sell sentiments. A wreath for eternity, a cross symbolic of Christianity. A vacant chair or a harp with a broken string symbolises a life cut off. A heart for love and a chaplet for military valour and victory. A sheaf or a posy for natural, uncontrived sadness plus, perhaps, many other ethnic interpretations.

The card, bearing the final message to a loved one, is, possibly, the most important element of any funeral tribute. Give it the respect it deserves by writing as neatly and clearly as you are able. The name of the deceased and the delivery address written on the reverse side will help both the funeral director and your driver.

Place the written card in a transparent envelope and seal it with Sellotape. Attach a covered wire (20G × 10″) (90 mm × 250 mm) using the method approved by your shop. Be sure that the card is firmly secured. Hook the free end of the wire to prevent it swivelling and insert it into the foam close to the spray, taking care not to unbalance the design. It must be prominently displayed above the flowers and tilted upwards for easy reading when viewed from above.

Every funeral tribute we produce is a challenge to our professional and creative skills. Our reward is the gratitude and appreciation shown by our satisfied customers.

Funeral posy

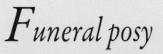

Although the funeral posy is usually chosen as a tribute to a young child, it is often the final tribute to a grandparent from the grandchildren. On occasions it is also selected by customers who are seeking a token of remembrance and respect which is neither too large or too expensive. It sometimes happens that the family and friends of the deceased ask that funeral flowers are taken to a hospital or old peoples' home after the burial service. Like the sympathy basket, the posy is particularly suitable for this purpose. As with other funeral designs, it is important that, on completion, the posy is viewed from above to ensure that it has an even, symmetrical, circular outline. **(See Plate 18.)**

——————— MATERIALS ———————

Suitable flowers: roses, carnations, freesia, spray chrysanthemums or any other small flowers
Suitable foliage: cupressus or leather leaf for the outline and ivy leaves or similar for the centre
Suitable container: a round, shallow dish or something similar

PREPARATION

Use sufficient foam to hold the quantity of flowers to be used. Anchor it securely to the container by taking a length of waterproof tape over the top surface of the foam, overlapping it and affixing it to the underside of the dish.

METHOD

1 Select flowers of colours that will blend and provide a variety of shapes and textures. Place in a container on a cleared work surface until ready for use.

FUNERAL TRIBUTES

Fig. 6.1

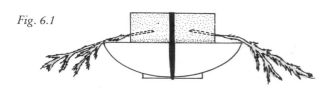

Fig. 6.2b

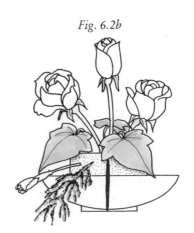

Keep turning to ensure even distribution

Fig. 6.2a

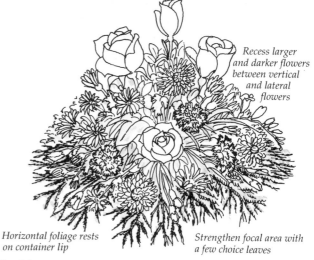

Recess larger and darker flowers between vertical and lateral flowers

Horizontal foliage rests on container lip

Strengthen focal area with a few choice leaves

Fig. 6.3

2 Cut the foliage stems diagonally with a sharp knife to produce an oblique point. Clean the lower 1½" (40 mm) of each stem of sideshoots and leaves.

3 Firmly insert the clean stems into the foam to a depth of 1½" (40 mm), low down in the sides of the foam and resting on the edge of the bowl, to form an even circle of foliage which flows over the sides of the container (*Fig. 6.1*).

4 The centre of the top of the foam will be the focal area. Strengthen it with a few choice leaves.

Mask the remaining visible foam with short pieces of foliage.

5 For the lateral placements, use flowers of the same length as those used for the verticals. Space them evenly around the edges of the foam to create the impression that they radiate from a central flower. Keep these lateral flower placements within the framework formed by the ring of foliage (*Fig. 6.2*). For the central flower, use a bud or a small flower, for a light and dainty effect (*Fig. 6.2*).

6 The area between the central flower and the lateral placements should be filled with selected flowers. Grade them so that buds are used around the outer ring and the size of the flowers increases towards the centre. The largest flowers of all should be recessed in the focal area to create a three dimensional effect. As you progress, keep turning the container so that all areas are worked evenly. (*Fig. 6.3*).

7 Place the finished design on the floor to check the overall shape.

8 Spray with water, using a fine mist sprayer.

9 If ribbon loops or bows are to be integrated into the design, use them with discretion to complement the chosen colour scheme.

10 The card is most important. Write it clearly and neatly, not forgetting the name of the deceased and the delivery address on the reverse.

11 Place the card in a clear plastic envelope and attach it with a covered wire to the focal area of the tribute where it can be read without difficulty.

*F*uneral spray

In many parts of the country the spray is the most popular of all funeral tributes. However, because the term 'spray' is so often misunderstood by the general public, it should be clearly explained to the customer when the order is being taken. One reason for its popularity lies in the fact that it can be produced to almost any size and from almost any selection of flowers and foliage. Although, generally, this design is chosen as one of the smaller tributes at a funeral, there are occasions when it is chosen by the principal mourners as the main tribute. In such cases the spray would lie on top of the coffin, in full view of the mourners and would be seen from many angles during the service, so a high level of design and workmanship is essential throughout.

MATERIALS

Suitable flowers: the choice of flowers is dependent upon customer preference, seasonal availability and the size of the tribute but only well conditioned and mature flowers should be used if the maximum effect is to be achieved
Suitable foliage: cupressus, hemlock, laurel, leather leaf or other seasonal foliage
Suitable container: several types of suitable container are available from small plastic sandwich trays to commercially produced, purpose made bases.

The chosen container should be rigid, easy to handle and provide the maximum support to the flowers and foliage. Cut a piece of foam large enough to hold the quantity of flowers to be used. Firmly anchor the foam to the container with two lengths of pot tape. Pass them over the top of the foam, overlap the ends and stick them securely to the underside of the container. The foam, which has been adequately soaked, can be positioned either centrally in the container or offset to one end.

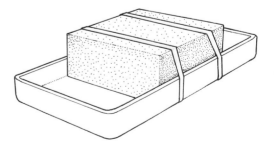

METHOD

1 Select the flowers and foliage for their colour and the variety of shapes and textures which they offer. To protect them from bruising and damage, place them in a vase or bucket until required.

2 Soak the foam and secure it to the container as described above.

3 Start with the foliage placements to outline the shape of the design and determine its size. Cut one piece to a length two thirds that of the planned overall length and another half the size of the first, or a third of the planned overall length. Sharpen both pieces to an oblique point. If the stems are woody pare away the stems to create flat surfaces on opposite sides at the base of the stem. This greatly reduces the risk of them twisting.

Remove sideshoots from the bottom two inches (50 mm) of the mainstem leaving a clean length to insert into the foam.

4 Insert each piece into either end of the foam, low down in its profile and resting on the edge of the container for support. The length of the design is now established.

5 Cut, trim and sharpen the two shorter pieces of foliage for the lateral foliage placements. Insert them centrally, either side of the foam, again, low down and resting on the lip of the container. The width of the finished design is now established.

6 Using more pieces of foliage of varying lengths, create a 'kite' shaped outline (*Fig. 6.4*).

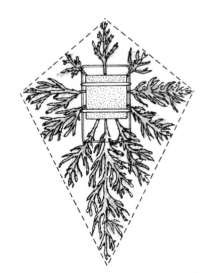

Fig. 6.4

7 Use more small foliage off-cuts to mask the remaining visible foam.

8 Now for the flower placements; when making them there are some general points to keep in mind:

- Flowers should be inserted into the foam at an angle so that the stems all appear to radiate from the focal area (*Figs. 6.5 and 6.6*).

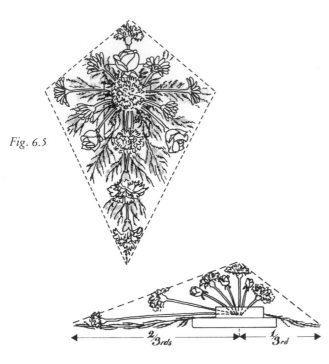

Fig. 6.5

Fig. 6.6 Profile and proportion

- Transition (grading the sizes of the flowers from the smaller to the larger) is achieved by using the flower heads low down in the sides of the foam but keeping within the outline formed by the foliage, and increasing their size progressively as the placements rise towards the top surface.

- The choice flowers are taken from one end of the design to the other with the height of the flowers increasing to a maximum in the focal area and then reducing.

- Using the sides of the foam, complete the design with the remaining flowers, recessing some to give depth and grouping them where possible to improve the overall effect.

9 Place the spray on the floor so that it can be viewed from above to check the outline shape. Adjust where necessary.

10 Spray with water, using a fine mist sprayer.

11 Since it bears the final message to a loved one, the card is a most important part of the tribute. Write it clearly and neatly, not forgetting the name of the deceased and the delivery address on the reverse.

See Plate 19, 20 and 20a

Double ended funeral spray

Although the double ended funeral spray (sometimes referred to as a 'coffin spray'), is suitable for almost any funeral, it is particularly appropriate when the close family of the deceased decide upon a single, collective tribute.

In such cases, as a main tribute, the double ended spray is carried on top of the coffin, in full view of the mourners. It is seen from many angles, so good design and finish are essential, particularly at the sides and ends of the tribute.

Although it can be made to any length, care must be taken to ensure that the overall height of a double ended spray can be accommodated within the hearse without damage.

If well designed this is a very beautiful and impressive tribute, but, like all funeral work it will be handled several times, so particular care must be taken to ensure that the flowers and foliage are anchored firmly in the foam if they are not to come adrift.

6

MATERIALS

Containers: a suitable, purpose-made foam base or, alternatively, any tray which will hold sufficient foam to support the quantity of flowers being used.

Suitable foliage: hemlock, cupressus and laurel are particularly suitable materials to establish the outline of the design. Eucalyptus or ruscus for example, can be used to advantage as decorative foliage and such boldly shaped leaves as dieffenbachia and hosta strengthen the focal area.

Suitable flowers: although flowers will generally be chosen to meet the requirements of the customer and preference will often be given to those which are in season, larger headed types such as carnations, gerberas, lilies and chrysanthemum blooms are, perhaps, more suitable for this design, although, because of their length, gladioli can be used with effect.

As with most funeral work, fully open, mature flowers which have been well conditioned will produce the maximum effect and ensure greater customer satisfaction. But whatever flowers are to be used choose them with colour blending in mind. A variety of shapes and textures will help to create a more interesting effect.

PREPARATION

If a purpose-made foam base is being used it should be well soaked without being over saturated. In the case of a tray, attach to it a generous amount of foam firmly secured by two or three lengths of pot tape, which should be taken over the foam, overlapped and secured to the underside of the tray.

The foam, as always should be adequately soaked but not to excess.

METHOD

1 Put the selected flowers and foliage into a bucket and place it on a clean, unobstructed work surface.

2 With a sharp knife, cut the first two pieces of outline foliage. As a guide, their combined lengths should equal the overall length of the finished design *when they are positioned in the foam.* Strip the lower ends of the stems and cut them to oblique points.

Note. If the stems are woody, pare opposite sides of the stems to produce flat surfaces. This will hold the stems firmly in the foam and prevent them twisting.

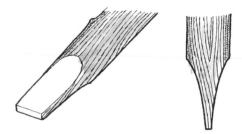

3 Insert the first two placements, one at each end of the foam block. Place them low down so that they rest on the lip of the container.

4 Cut two pieces of foliage of equal length for the sides. Push them into the foam on opposite sides to establish the overall width. Again, they should rest on the lip of the container.

5 From the basic shape, form a diamond by further placements of shorter pieces of foliage, inserted low down in the profile of the foam as were the earlier placements (*Fig. 6.7*).

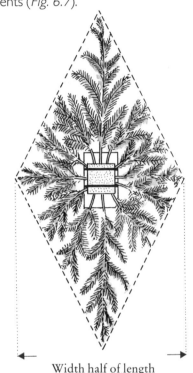

Width half of length

Fig. 6.7

6 Using the flowers selected for the outline of the design, follow the lines of the foliage, turning the container from time to time to ensure that the flowers are evenly placed on all sides. It is important that these placements are made so that the angle of the stems appears to be flowing from the focal area of the spray.

7 Using the choice flowers, work from each end of the spray towards the middle, gradually increasing their height as you progress until a maximum is reached at the focal area at the centre of the design (*Fig. 6.8*).

Fig. 6.8 Profile

8 Place larger or darker flowers below the level of the choice flowers to achieve recession.

9 Larger leaves in the centre of the spray will strengthen the focal area.

10 The grouping of flowers will improve the overall effect and create interest in the design.

11 To further conceal any exposed foam, use decorative foliage between the flower placements, being sure to keep within the overall diamond shape.

12 Check that no foam is visible.

13 Place the finished spray on the floor and view it from above to check that the regular diamond shape has been retained throughout.

14 Spray with water from a fine mist sprayer.

15 Since it bears the last greetings to a loved one, the card is a most important part of the spray. Write it clearly and neatly. The name of the deceased and the delivery address, written clearly on the reverse of the card will assist the funeral director and your delivery driver.

16 Place the card in a cellophane envelope to protect it from flower moisture and rain and fix it by covered wire near the focal area of the spray where it can be easily read.

*F*uneral sheaf

The sheaf is one of our loveliest funeral tributes. For many florists it is also one of the most challenging. Well designed and skilfully executed, its beauty will always be appreciated by your customer, so the time and effort taken in mastering the necessary technique will be well rewarded. When recommending a sheaf to a customer, never propose it as a cheap alternative.

The sheaf derives its name from a sheaf of corn which, in many respects, it resembles. It is an arrangement of flowers and foliage, a tied bunch on natural stems, forward facing and designed with a 'profile' which increases in depth towards the place where the stems come together and are secured; the 'tying point'. Below this point, the stems, with foliage removed, are allowed to fan out naturally and are long enough to balance the sheaf and create a 'return end'.

MATERIALS

All the materials used in creating a sheaf should be well conditioned.

Foliage: all should be of adequate length. Beech, spruce, hemlock, laurel and pittosporum are all suitable.
The flowers selected should reflect the function which they are required to fulfil. For example,
Flowers for length: iris, stocks, gladioli or similar
Flowers for width, recession and transition: spray chrysanthemums, spray carnations, narcissi etc.
Flowers for interest and value: carnations, roses
Ribbon: 2″ (50 mm) in toning colours
Twine or similar for tying, Polytie or narrow ribbon, for example.

PREPARATION

The construction of a sheaf requires strong pieces of backing foliage, evenly balanced on each side of a straight, central stem.

For the spine of the sheaf, which will provide the necessary strength and support, select a well shaped piece of foliage of the same proposed overall length as the completed sheaf. Alternatively, combine two or more pieces. We are seeking to create a strong, straight, central backbone to support the finished design.

Shorter pieces of foliage will be required to establish the width and outline. Remove leaves and thorns from the lower end of the flower stems, below where you estimate the tying point will be.

METHOD

1 Start with the foliage spine and add front flowers (*Fig. 6.9*).

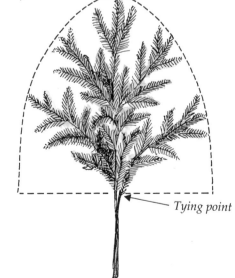

Tying point

Fig. 6.9   Tying point – all flowers and foliage radiate from this point

2 Commencing at the tip, with the longer flowers and working downwards and outwards add more flowers, supplementing them with foliage to create a foliage outline which will extend about 2″ (50 mm) beyond the outermost flower placement (*Fig. 6.10*).

Bow conceals tie point

Fig. 6.10 Start at the tip and work down towards tie point, keeping the outline in mind all the time

3 All stems must meet at the tying point and be allowed to fan out naturally.

4 Build the design as you progress, introducing selected flowers to the tying point at the centre of the widest part of the design.

5 Small sprigs of foliage can be added between the flower stems at the tying point to both build the profile and prevent the stems from slipping.

6 Ideally, the sheaf should be completed before tying. Take a piece of the tying material – sufficient to pass twice around the assembled stems plus a bit more to make it easier to handle and manipulate.
Fold it into two equal lengths. Pass the two cut ends around the sheaf and through the loop and pull tight. Pass the two ends around the sheaf in opposite directions, bring them together and knot them securely (*Fig. 6.11*). Cut off surplus material.

Fig. 6.11

7 Alternatively, the sheaf can be tied as it is being put together. Tie one end of the tying material to the main foliage stem, the spine, at the spot where you estimate the tying point will be and tie in the flowers and foliage as you assemble them. Do not use more than one turn for every one or two stems and *take care to concentrate the tying point in one place. Do not let it wander.*

8 From the ribbon you have selected, make a bow of a size appropriate to the design and attach it to a length of narrow ribbon of the same colour.

9 Attach the bow securely to conceal the tying point.

10 Finally, trim off the ends of the stems diagonally at varying lengths to create an attractive appearance.

See Plates 21 and 21a

Sympathy basket

The sympathy basket, or cremation basket as it is sometimes called, is a tribute which can be suggested to a customer for any funeral. As the family and friends of the deceased often ask for funeral flowers to be taken to a hospital or old people's home after the service, the sympathy basket can be recommended as particularly suitable for this purpose. On the other hand, a sympathy basket, given to the bereaved as a token of condolence is sometimes more appropriate than a tribute to the deceased. The sympathy basket is, generally, a balanced design with the focal area located beneath the handle. But it should be remembered that it is carried by the handle, so care must be taken to ensure that there is no likelihood of any of the flowers in the area of the handle being damaged. As with funeral floristry generally, the best effect is created if well conditioned, fully open, mature flowers are used.

MATERIALS

The basket: the most suitable baskets are rectangular or oval in shape with either a stitched in, soft plastic liner or a rigid, detachable insert. In either case it is essential that the liner is undamaged and watertight.
Suitable foliage: hemlock and leather leaf for the outline with large ivy, or similar leaves to add visual weight to the focal area with such foliage as eucalyptus or similar to lighten the design and complement the flowers.
Suitable flowers: the choice of flowers will usually be determined by the season of the year and customer

6

FUNERAL TRIBUTES

preference, but whatever the choice, care must be taken to blend their colours and ensure that the variety of shapes and textures contribute to the design.

Preparing the basket

Cut a piece of foam large enough to support the quantity of flowers to be used. It should be thick enough to protrude about one inch above the rim of the basket to allow room for the lateral placements of both flowers and foliage. Secure the foam to the container. If the basket has a stitched in liner use pot tape or cellotwist stretched from one side of the basket, where the handle joins the body, to the other. It should be stretched tightly enough so that it cuts lightly into the foam to prevent any movement. If the basket has a detachable liner, secure the foam to the centre of the liner with either pot tape of cellotwist. Then, fix the liner to the basket by the same means. The foam, as always, should be adequately soaked.

1″
(*25 mm*)

—————— METHOD ——————

1 Select the flowers and foliage, place them in a vase or bucket to protect them and place it on a clean, uncluttered work bench.

2 With a sharp knife, cut two pieces of the outline foliage, hemlock, for example, to the same length, cutting the stems diagonally to form an oblique point. Remove the lower leaves and sideshoots so that there is sufficient clean stem to be pushed into the foam to hold it securely.

3 Insert the cleaned stems into either end of the foam, angling them downwards so that they rest on the lip of the basket with the tips of the foliage touching the work surface. By so placing the foliage, the design will be given soft flowing lines (*Fig. 6.12a*).

4 Cut two shorter pieces of foliage to a length roughly a quarter of the planned overall length of the design. These will be the first lateral placements which are inserted into the foam at the points where the handle joins the sides of the basket. As with the first foliage placements, they should be angled downwards towards the workbench.

The first four foliage placements should form an elongated diamond shape. (*See Fig. 6.12b overleaf.*)

Fig. 6.12a   Angle foliage downwards to touch working surface

*Build flowers up in height
to group below handle,
leaving space for carrying*

5 Remaining within this basic outline, make further placements of short pieces of foliage to enhance and protect the flowers.

6 Mask the exposed foam with short pieces of foliage, using larger leaves below the handle to establish a focal area.

7 Cut the stems of some of the smaller headed flowers diagonally and insert them round all sides of the foam, following the outline formed by foliage. These placements must be inserted at an angle so that they appear to radiate from the focal area of the design. (*Refer again to Fig. 6.12b*).

that of the main flowers, create recession and bring about a three dimensional effect.

10 Check that all areas of the foam are concealed and that none of the mechanics of the basket's construction can be seen.

11 Spray with water, using a fine mist sprayer.

12 Write the message clearly and neatly on the face of the card, bearing in mind that it is the final greeting to a loved one. On the reverse side of the card write the name of the deceased and the delivery address to assist the funeral director and your driver.

13 Place the card in a cellophane envelope to protect it. Fix it firmly to a covered wire and attach it to the tribute, near the focal area, where it can be easily seen.

See Plate 22

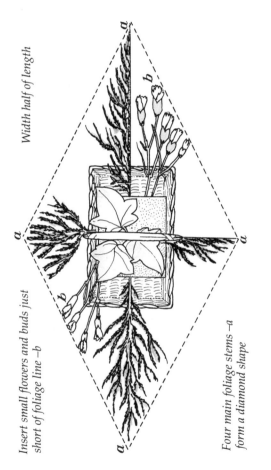

Width half of length

b

a

Insert small flowers and buds just short of foliage line –b

Four main foliage stems –a form a diamond shape

Fig. 6.12b

8 Working from each end towards the focal area, insert the main flowers, raising them progressively until they reach their maximum height at the focal area.

9 Choice flowers should be grouped below the handle, but sufficient space must be left to allow the basket to be carried without damaging them. Larger flowers or those of a darker colour, used at a lower level than

Open wreath

The open wreath is probably our most traditional funeral tribute. It was developed from a natural garland of flowers interwoven to make a circle, symbolising eternity or endless remembrance. A well designed open wreath is a blend of flowers, evenly spaced and with a variety of foliage interspersed between them to create a textural effect.

MATERIALS

A foam wreath base, ideally not less than 12″ (300 mm) in diameter. Other sizes are available, ranging from 10″ (250 mm) to 18″ (450 mm).
Suitable foliage: cupressus, boxwood, beech, mahonia and spruce are all suitable. They should be mixed to add variety and interest to the design. Foliage also serves to cover the mechanics of the construction.
Suitable flowers: in an open wreath flowers of widely differing shapes and textures are brought together to create interest in the design. The triangular outline of the iris, the rounded form and tweedy texture of the carnation, the rose with its satin like sheen and distinctive shape and the daisy eye feature of single AYR chrysanthemums can all be combined with smaller flowers such as sweet peas, gypsophila and pinks to bring about transition or movement in the design.

Colours should be chosen to harmonise and create an effect which is both interesting and pleasing.

PREPARATION

Trim the square edges from the base with a sharp knife or rub them off. Moisten the base sufficiently to sustain the flowers, taking care not to soften it by oversoaking, thus making it difficult to secure the stems.

Prepare foliage for the edging by trimming it to a suitable length to allow it to extend over the outer edge of the base. Cut the foliage stem on an oblique angle and remove enough foliage from the cut end to permit 1½" (40 mm) of clean stem to be inserted into the foam.

The length of these side foliage placements should be slightly greater than that of the flowers intended for outline.

METHOD

1 Push the clean foliage stems firmly into the outer edge of the foam, low down, close to the base and sloping slightly downwards to conceal the plastic foundation. These placements should be dense enough to provide a protective background to the flowers which will follow.

2 Repeat this operation on the inside of the ring, this time angling them 45° *upwards*. Use a selection of the other foliages to conceal the foam base and generally add interest to the finished wreath.

3 Select five of the choice flowers, roses or carnations for example, and, after carefully judging the correct length (about 5" (125 mm) for a 12" (300 mm) ring), cut the stems obliquely and clean the lower 1½" (40 mm) of stem. Insert them evenly around the top of the foam, so that they are equally spaced, upright and

securely anchored. These flowers form the main area of focal attraction and establish the height of the tribute. Their placement must be planned with the completed wreath in mind.

4 Outward facing flowers, the lateral placements, are inserted low down in the foam, close to and within the foliage outline to form a near circle (*Fig. 6.13*).

Space five main choice flowers equally around the base

A variety of blended foliage should be used to conceal the base

Fig. 6.13

Place lateral flowers within the foliage line

5 A similar ring of flowers is placed around the inner edge of the base, but angled upwards at an angle of 45°, as were the inner foliage placements. The outline of the wreath is now established.

6 Select five choice flowers of a different type from those used for the earlier vertical placements described in point 3. This creates variety within the design. After cutting the stems to a length of about 5" (125 mm), insert them into the foam vertically and intersperse them evenly between the choice flowers used earlier.

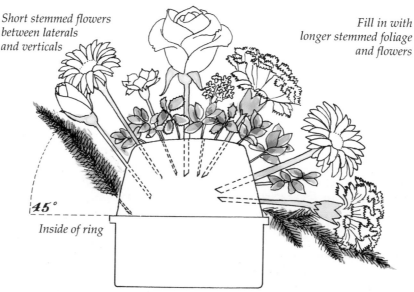

Short stemmed flowers between laterals and verticals

Fill in with longer stemmed foliage and flowers

45°

Inside of ring

Section through wreath

7 Between the inner and outer rings, place short stemmed flowers, recessed close to the foam.

8 Fill out the design with longer stemmed flowers, interspersing transitional flowers between them to achieve a well rounded finish to the design.

9 Check the finished wreath from all angles, not forgetting to view it from above. Add further flower material if required so that the profile is well rounded and the wreath forms as perfect a circle as you can achieve.

10 Spray with water.

11 After inscribing the card neatly and clearly, place it in a cellophane envelope and attach it to the wreath with a taped wire.

See Plates 23, 23a, 23b, 23c, 23d and 23e

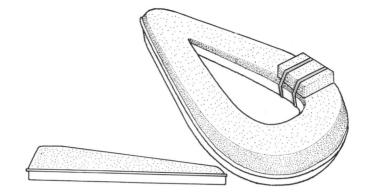

Foliage based chaplet

This design dates from ancient times when heroes were crowned with laurel. In those days the leaves of the bay tree were used, this is reflected in the tree's latin name, *Laurus nobilis*. Even to this day chaplets are particularly appropriate for military funerals. **(See Plate 24.)** Memorial designs also, are usually in chaplet form.

MATERIALS

Foam chaplet base
Laurel, camellia or similar foliage
One third of a block of foam
Fixing tape
'German' pins
Suitable flowers for spray: bold types of flowers are usually used, for example, carnations, roses, etc. Wherever possible use the natural foliage of the flowers to conceal the mechanics of the design.

METHOD

1 Fix the foam block to the base with two lengths of waterproof tape, overlapping them beneath the base. Take care to position the block far enough from the rounded end, or butt of the design to prevent damage to the flowers in the spray should the chaplet be propped up.

2 Because the chaplet is an almost flat design, the thickness of the foam can be reduced evenly by tapering it from the thickest part in the spray area to the thinnest, at the point.

3 Chamfer the inner and outer edges of the foam base, either with a sharp knife or by rubbing it away with your fingers. Taking care not to oversoak it, wet the foam sufficiently to sustain the flower material.

4 To prepare the leaves of the foliage, remove them from the main stem and clean them with a damp cloth. Discard any which are damaged, deformed or otherwise blemished. Grade the remaining leaves according to their size. The smaller ones will be used at the point of the chaplet and the larger leaves at the rounded end.

Starting from the tip, pin the leaves to the foam base, using the smaller leaves first and increasing their size as you progress towards the rounded end of the design.

5 All the leaves must point towards the tip of the chaplet. Continue working down the frame, covering it to form a fish scale pattern.

Tip

Start at the tip with smaller leaves, gradually getting larger towards the round end

*Fig. 6.14   * The point of each leaf must line up with the outer edge of each leaf just laid*

Because the size of the leaves you are using will increase as you work from the tip downwards, it follows that the width of the design will increase automatically towards the rounded end (*Fig. 6.14*).

To create and maintain a neat outline, the point, or tip, of a lower leaf should be aligned with the outer edge of the upper leaf which precedes it.

The spray

The spray must be in proportion to the finished design, not less than one third of the overall size. Insert the stem of the longest flower at least 1½″ (40 mm) low down, into the end of the foam block in order to secure it firmly.

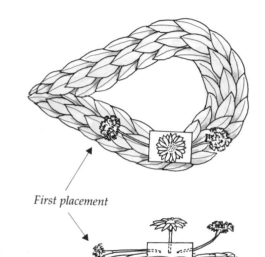

First placement

Fig. 6.15

This first placement should lie along the base with the flower facing towards the tip (*Fig. 6.15*).

The remaining flowers should be positioned at varying levels to form a spray which conforms roughly to the shape of the base. The height of the spray should rise towards its centre, where flowers are also recessed to strengthen the design and form a focal point.

The spray must be carefully balanced and integrated into the overall design of the chaplet and not appear to be 'falling off' the base.
Conceal the mechanics, preferably with foliage from the flowers used in the spray.

Spray the design with water and attach the card, taking care not to destroy the overall balance of the chaplet. It is emphasised that the card plays a particularly important role in funeral work. Neatness, legibility and absolute clarity are essential.

Ribbon edging

It is customary for most funeral designs to have an edging which protrudes beyond the base and extends a short distance beyond the flowers to protect them from damage and provide a background.

Traditionally, a foliage edging is used. In the case of loose or open designs it often consists of cupressus or another tough foliage, whereas with based designs a more formal edging such as, ivy, camelia or similar attractive leaves may be more appropriate.

Alternatively, an attractive edging can be created from ribbon, particularly with based designs. Although this method may have limitations because of the ribbon's limited width, it should be pointed out that it is possible to widen the ribbon by glueing or stapling two pieces together.

For everyday work, standard 2″ (50 mm) polypropylene ribbon is generally used but other types can be called upon depending upon the design to be created. For example, in the case of a textured design, hessian ribbon may be more suitable, whereas in a tribute for a girl or young woman, synthetic lace could be better.

Whatever type of ribbon is chosen, it should be pleated for both the decorative effect and the extra strength that it gives.
There are two types of pleating in everyday use:

Single pleating, where the ribbon is folded onto itself at regular intervals of 1–2″ (25–50 mm) to create a ripple effect and *Box pleating*, where alternate pleats are reversed to create a box-like effect. Both types are described.

Single pleating

The width of each pleat must be regular and even. A more pleasing effect is achieved if the pleats are not creased or flattened.

─────── MATERIALS ───────

Clean, sharp ribbon scissors
Stapler and staples
Glue gun
1½″ (40 mm) pins or 'German pins'
Blunt ended knife
2″ (50 mm) ribbon

Note. The length of ribbon required is dependent upon the size of the tribute and the type. For example, for a wreath or posy pad, only one length is needed. A heart calls for two lengths, one for each half of the tribute, the direction of the pleats being reversed for the second half.

For a cross, because the pleating must flow from the axis towards the tip of each limb, eight pieces of ribbon are required, plus four box pleats to cover the ends. In all cases 3" (75 mm) of unpleated ribbon should be left at the end of each run.

METHOD

Note. These instructions assume the florist to be right handed. Should this not be the case, reverse them.

1 Leaving the ribbon attached to the roll, pull off a length and hold it between the thumb and forefinger of your left hand with the cut end facing away from you.

2 With your right hand, push forward enough ribbon beneath your left thumb to form a pleat with the length of ribbon attached to the roll uppermost. Keep the edges of the ribbon exactly in line with each other.

3 Staple across the end of each pleat ¼" (5 mm) from the edge and parallel to it. (Fig. 6.16).

4 Continue the process, making pleats at intervals of 1–2" (20–40 mm), depending upon the effect required.

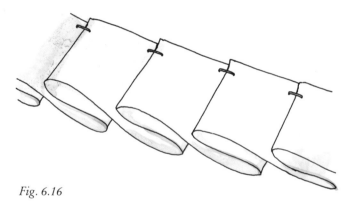

Fig. 6.16

Box pleating

METHOD

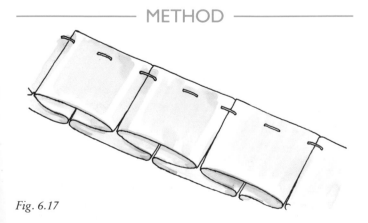

Fig. 6.17

1 Make a pleat as described in point 2 above and staple it.

2 Turn the first pleat towards you and make another in the opposite direction. The edges should be parallel and touching.

3 Staple across the end of each pleat and in the centre so that each fold is stapled and securely held (Fig. 6.17).

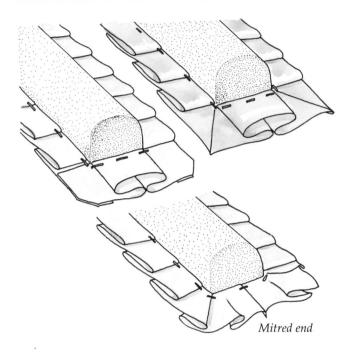

Mitred end

Attaching the ribbon

METHOD

Ribbon is attached to a *foam base* either with pins or by a glue gun. If pins are used follow this procedure, but for added security, first run adhesive tape around the foam immediately above the rigid plastic base and push the pins through the tape and into the foam (Fig. 6.18).

With pins:

Either 1½" (40 mm) pins or 'German' pins are used to attach ribbon to a mossed base. Keep the ribbon close to the base of the frame and push in the pins diagonally and angled slightly upwards about 1" (25 mm) apart.

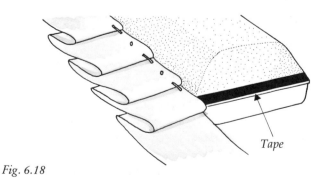

Tape

Fig. 6.18

Glueing the ribbon:

1 Using a knife, make a groove round the edge of the foam, just above its base and remove any loose particles.

2 Run a liberal seam of glue along the groove and the exposed lip of the plastic base. From the first pleat, extend the stapled edge of the pleated ribbon along the glue and press it home firmly with the knife blade (*Fig. 6.19*).

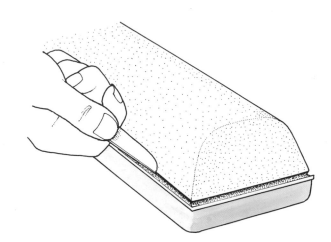

Fig. 6.19   Make a groove with your knife and glue along it in 12″ (300 mm) stages

3 Continue in 12″ (300 mm) stages around the base.

4 For a circular base, work around the perimeter of the frame and finish off neatly.

5 For a heart shaped base, begin in the cleft and run the ribbon round each side to the point. With single pleating, the pleats should point downwards towards the point (*Fig. 6.20*).

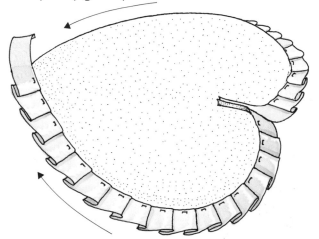

Fig. 6.20   Cut 2″ (50 mm) groove in the cleft to take the ribbon-work from this point towards the tip

6 The corners of ribbon edged cushions are finished in the same manner.

7 In a cross, the pleats flow from the centre. To complete the ends of the limbs, use a short length of ribbon to form a single box pleat, the same width as the base of the cross with 3″ (75 mm) of free ribbon at each end.

8 Attach the single box pleat centrally to the end of the limb and mitre the join, as described previously or overlap the end and side ribbons to form a square join. Glue, or staple them together and trim to make a neat end.

9 Should you wish to have rounded ends to the cross, round off the ends of the foam on each limb and extend the pleats to a single mitred joint in the centre.

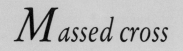

Massed cross

A massed or based cross is usually requested as a special tribute from a close relative of the deceased or collectively from a family group. For Christians, of course, the shape is both traditional and symbolic.

Foam bases for crosses are available in lengths varying from 2′ to 5′ (60 cm to 150 cm). Preformed extensions are available from some manufacturers.

Symmetry and a cleanly defined outline are essential attributes of the design. The massed cross can be edged with either ribbon or foliage.

A spray, or cluster, is positioned at the junction of the arms of the cross, either parallel to them or diagonally across them. In either case, the spray should be at least one third of the overall size of the cross, well balanced on the base and moulded to conform to the contours of the design.

MATERIALS

Cross base
Part of a block of foam for the spray
Fixing tape
Stapler/staples
2″ (50 mm) ribbon
German pins
Glue gun
Flowers for base: double AYR are ideal. Carnations, stocks, hydrangeas, violets or any flowers which can be massed to produce a textured, velvet-like finish are suitable.
Flowers for the spray: distinctive, choice flowers. For example, roses, carnations, gerberas alone or together with spray carnations, dendrobiums, lily of the valley may all be suitable.

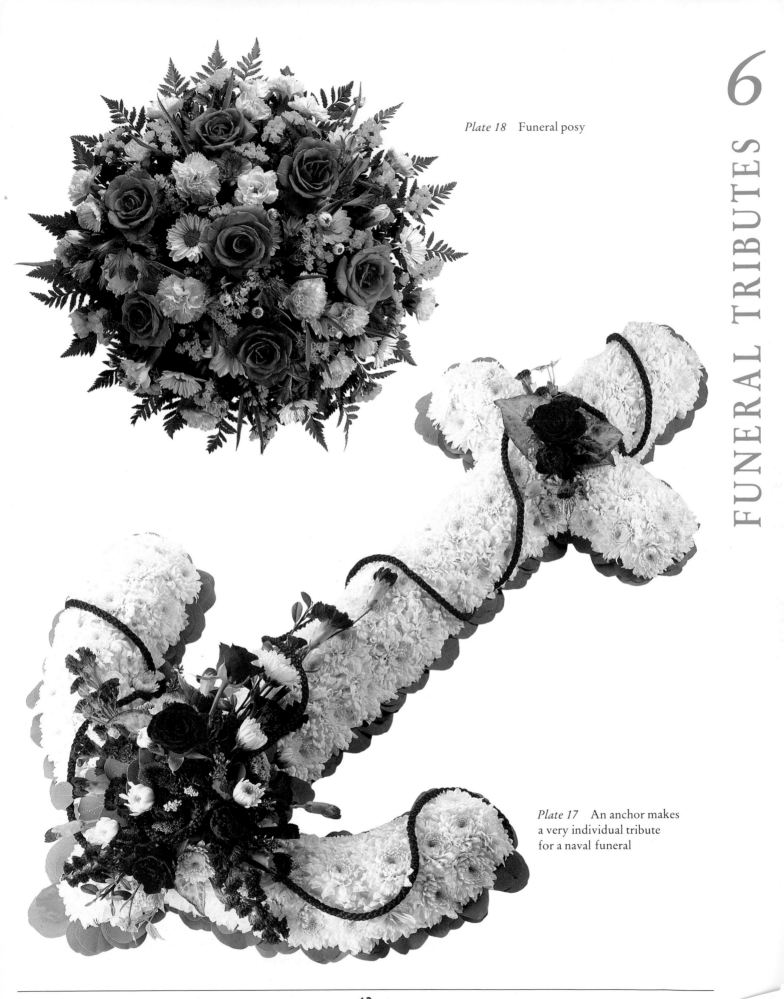

Plate 18   Funeral posy

Plate 17   An anchor makes
a very individual tribute
for a naval funeral

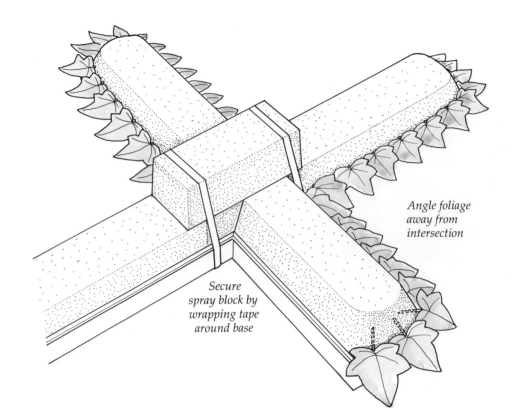

Angle foliage away from intersection

Secure spray block by wrapping tape around base

METHOD

1 The base on which the spray will be made is secured firmly to the base at the intersection of the vertical and horizontal arms of the cross. For a 33" (830 mm) base, one third of a block of foam is sufficient. It should be high enough to protrude about 1" (25 mm) above the level of the base of flowers.

2 Chamfer the edges of the block and tidy the ends. Secure it to the cross at the intersection of the arms with two pieces of waterproof tape, one above the intersection and the other below. Wrap them completely around the base. Pull them tight enough to hold the block securely, overlap the ends and stick them to the underside of the base.

3 If foliage edging is to be used moisten the base thoroughly without oversoaking it.

METHOD

1 Trim the foliage to allow at least 1½" (40 mm) of clean stem to insert into the foam. Cut the ends diagonally to obtain a sharp point.

2 Insert each piece at an angle, sloping it away from the intersections of the arms and downwards to conceal the plastic base.

3 The ends of the limbs can be square or rounded but care must be taken to ensure that they are all of equal width when finished.

Note. Edging with ribbon is described in the section Ribbon Edging (see page 60).

The flower base

Edging

Depending upon the customer's preference, the cross can be edged with either ribbon or foliage.

Edging with foliage: on a 33" (830 mm) base the foliage edging should extend about 1" (25 mm) beyond the base of flowers and the flowers themselves about 1" (25 mm) above the foam. These measurements will vary according to the size of the base being used but they must be in proportion.

METHOD

1 Cut the flower stems obliquely to allow 1½" (40 mm) of clean stem to push into foam. *Do not cut the stems too short.*

2 Position your body so that your head is directly above the cross. Working along each limb of the base, and towards yourself, place the centre run of flowers in the middle of the foam. These placements establish the height of the flower base. Each flower should be

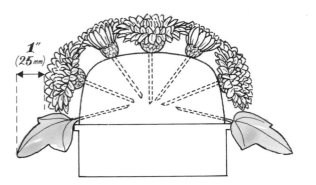

Fig. 6.21   Fill any gaps with small flowers or buds

touching its neighbours without crowding or overlapping them (*Fig. 6.21*).

3 Continue with the outer lines of flowers, making sure that they fit snugly against the edging material. The placement of these three rows of base flowers should produce a domed profile and an even, velvet like texture.

4 Any gaps should be filled with surplus buds and small florets.

5 When all four limbs on the cross are completed, raise it to eye level and look both along its length and along the arms to ensure that the height and width are consistent throughout (*Fig. 6.22*).

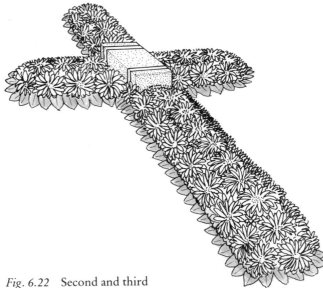

Fig. 6.22   Second and third rows should fit snugly, just touching but not overlapping

6 Check the overall shape by placing the cross on the floor and viewing it from above.

The spray on a massed cross

The spray, or cluster, is the focal point of the cross and is positioned at the intersection of its four limbs. A guideline to the spray's proportion is for it to be at least one third the overall length of the tribute. Two thirds of the length of the spray lies below the focal point and one third above.

The width of the spray should be two thirds of its length. Although the height of the spray may be up to one half of its width, this dimension may have to be reduced in the case of a coffin cross to avoid damage to the flowers (*Figs. 6.23* and *6.24*).

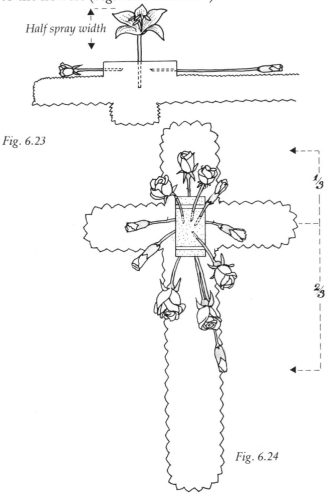

Half spray width

Fig. 6.23

Fig. 6.24

Carry out a final check on the finished cross in detail and make any necessary adjustments.

Spray with water.

Complete the card neatly and legibly, not forgetting the name of the deceased and the delivery address on the reverse.

Enclose the card in a transparent envelope and attach it by covered wire to the spray, taking care not to bruise any flowers or unbalance the design.

See Plates 25, 25a and 25b

Plate 19   Funeral spray

Plate 20   Double ended funeral spray

Plate 20a   Double ended
funeral spray

Plate 21   Funeral sheaf

Plate 21a   Lily funeral sheaf

Plate 22   Sympathy basket

The spray on massed tributes

The spray, or cluster, in a floral tribute is the focus of attention when that piece of work is being viewed. So it is important that the design, proportion and placement of the sprays are perfect.

The spray is an arrangement of flowers so the design principles which are involved follow rules described in the Design in Floristry section (chapter 4) of this manual.

Proportion is to some extent determined by the size and type of tribute, but a general guideline is that the size of the spray should not be less than one third that of the overall area of the base. Careful placement will ensure that the completed tribute is balanced and looks right.

On a cross the spray will usually be placed at the intersection. It may extend in line with the length of the cross, be diagonal to it, or curved, but in each case the focal point of the spray will be balanced directly above the junction of the cross.

On a wreath the spray may follow the curve of the ring, or lie across it but it must be balanced with the focal point above the base and not appear to be 'falling off' it.

On a cushion, pillow or heart the spray is tailored to suit the shape of the base and usually placed offset from the centre to balance the total design and provide a motif to enliven the base.

Cushion heart

This beautiful formal tribute is chosen to express love and affection for a member of the family or a very dear friend. It can be made in a variety of sizes. The choice of materials used can often reflect the personality or interests of the deceased.

Ribbon or foliage edged, the heart can be based with a variety of materials, usually round headed flowers, or varieties which can be massed to give a soft, cushion-like effect. More distinction can be given to the design, by moulding the massed flower base to achieve a cleft at the centre line.

A flower spray to complement the base and edging, integrates the design into a complete picture.

MATERIALS

Foam frame: a proprietory base, or one cut to the correct shape and size from designer foam
suitable edging: pleated ribbon, ivy, cupressus
suitable flowers for the base: spray chrysanthemums, carnations, hydrangeas, scabious, sweet williams, dahlias
Flowers for the spray: roses, carnations, lilies, gerberas, freesias, spray carnations. All of a size proportionate to the size of the base
Suitable foliage for the flower spray: small hosta, ivy, dieffenbachia

METHOD

1 Chamfer the edges of the foam and cut a groove, approximately 2″ (50 mm) long between the curves at the top of the frame to make a cleft in the centre of the frame (*Fig. 6.25*).

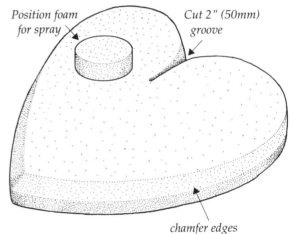

Position foam for spray

Cut 2″ (50mm) groove

chamfer edges

Fig. 6.25

2 The foam should be adequately soaked. If ribbon is to be glued, this should be done after the ribbon has been attached (see page 60 on Ribbon Edging).

3 Start the edging where the central cleft begins. It is immaterial whether the pleats face away from the starting point or towards it. Continue round the curve to the point at the bottom of the frame and cut the ribbon, leaving about 3″ (75 mm) of unpleated ribbon to allow for a mitred finish.

4 Repeat on the opposite side of the frame, starting from the top of the cleft, making sure that the pleats *face in the same direction as those on the other side of the frame*. Again, leave about 3″ (75 mm) of unpleated ribbon to complete the mitred finish (*Fig. 6.26*).

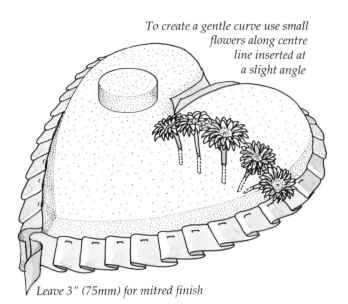

To create a gentle curve use small flowers along centre line inserted at a slight angle

Leave 3" (75mm) for mitred finish

Fig. 6.26   Note proportion and shape

Fig. 6.27   Pin or glue pleated ribbon

5 For the flower spray; using wire pegs or glue, attach a piece of foam to one side of the heart, at its widest part, making sure it is firmly secured.

6 Select the materials to be used and keep them in a bucket of water. When using basing flowers with heads of different sizes, grade them and use the smaller flowers on the outer edge, progressing to the larger ones in the middle of the design. For a more distinctive effect, mould the heart so that the flower base rises in a gentle curve from the outer edge and dips into a cleft at the centre. Keep the line of the cleft straight, following an imaginary line from a central point between the curves at the top of the design to the point at the bottom.

7 The flower stems should be cut diagonally and should be long enough to allow sufficient measure to be pushed into the foam securely.

8 When massing, the flower heads on the outer edges should just touch the edging material. There should be no spaces between the flowers. The pins which secure the ribbon edging – if they are used – should be concealed by the flowers. A smooth even finish is to be achieved (*Fig. 6.27*).

9 The spray, although an integral part of the base, should only appear to be resting lightly on it. The flowers and foliage of which the spray is composed, should be kept within the outline of the tribute to echo its finished shape.

10 Check that all the mechanics are concealed, spray with a fine mister and place the card in the spray near the focal flowers, where it can be easily seen by the mourners.

See Plate 26

Plate 23   Open wreath

Plate 23a   Massed wreath with ribbon edging

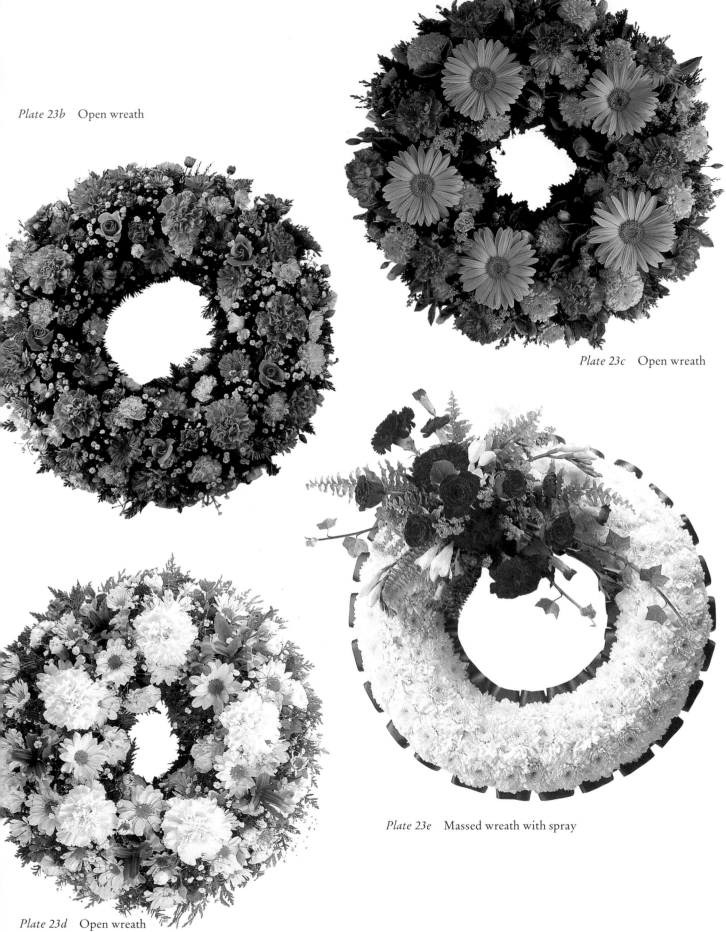

Plate 23b   Open wreath

Plate 23c   Open wreath

Plate 23e   Massed wreath with spray

Plate 23d   Open wreath

*I*ntroduction

Floristry is constantly changing and progressing. The development of new techniques means that a keen designer needs to keep an open mind, ever ready to adopt a new method which may prove to be more efficient or commercially economical. The use of foam bases is now widely accepted and offers many advantages, including speed, ease of use, moisture retention, cleanliness, and the almost complete elimination of wiring.

However, it is advisable for students of the trade to perfect designing on moss before attempting to design on foam bases as their use demands care, attention to detail, and the development of a sound technique.

*O*pen wreath on moss

An open or loose wreath is a descriptive name for a circle of flowers representing eternity or endless remembrance. The centre, therefore, must never be filled in. The flowers are arranged with foliage between them, and varied for interest. They also serve to cover the mechanics. Flowers may be recessed or elevated and mixed or grouped tastefully, but each one should be distinctly visible.

MATERIALS

Mossed wreath frame preferably not less than 12"
(300 mm) diameter.
Wreath wrap
Flowers and foliage: for suitable flowers and foliages, refer to those suggested for the 'open wreath on foam base' p. 57.

PREPARATION

Clean and tease out the damp moss. Moss the frame firmly. Clearly define the outline. The moss should be of a resilient texture and of an even depth.

Use twine or wire taking care not to overbind the frame. The finished frame should be well padded, full and firm so that the materials can be securely anchored.

*M*ossing a wreath frame

Mossing is the first step in the preparation of a wreath.

METHOD

1 Tease the damp moss and remove any other material (*Fig. 7.1*).

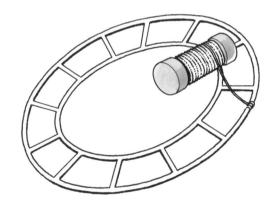

Fig. 7.1   Tease out moss removing all rubbish

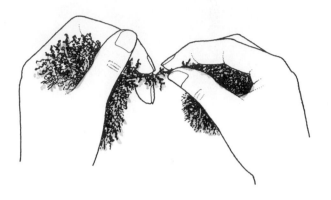

Fig. 7.2   Tie start point wire to outer edge

2 Take the wreath frame and tie the string or wire to its outer ring (*Fig. 7.2*).

3 Take hold of two handfuls of moss. Compress the moss to fit the width of the wreath frame (*Fig. 7.3*).

Fig. 7.3   Compress moss to the same width as frame

Fig. 7.4

4 Place the compressed moss on the frame and bind it down firmly, taking care to leave about 1″ (25 mm) space between the binding loops (*Fig. 7.4*).
Tuck each fresh handful of moss partly under the previous handful so as to ensure:
  • firmness
  • evenness
  • depth
Continue this process all around the frame, then cut the wire or string and tie securely.
Tidy the frame by trimming off any surplus moss.

5 Foliage or polythene can be used to neatly finish the tribute. It should be used economically to completely cover the back and extend 1″ (25 mm) up over the sides. It needs to be well anchored so that no mossy gaps are visible.

Greening a wreath frame

Once the frame has been properly mossed, you can proceed with greening it.

Foliage edging

Pieces must be of uniform size and content, with well fan-shaped sprays. Mounts should be constructed neatly and firmly by either the single or double-leg method. If the double-leg method is used, an adequate length of wire must be left to permit a firm anchorage.

The gauge of wire selected should be suitable for the type of foliage chosen; too fine a gauge will not support the foliage nor give firm anchorage in the moss. The foliage should be inserted into the moss so that it lies at an angle to the base since it is to form a border to the design as well as providing protection

for the flowers. Avoid large floppy pieces which will drop away from the frame and look untidy (See figs 7.5 to 7.14).

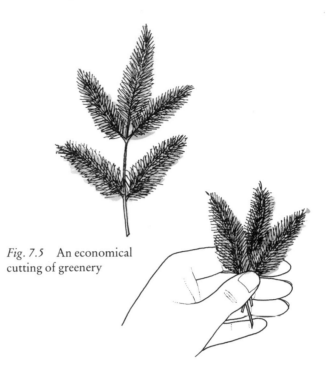

Fig. 7.5   An economical cutting of greenery

Fig. 7.6   A selection of pieces, showing suitable shapes and sizes

Fig. 7.7   Single-leg mounting of greenery

Fig. 7.8   Double-leg mounting of greenery

Fig. 7.11   The positioning of single-leg mounted pieces

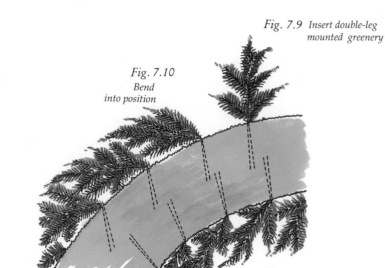

Fig. 7.9   Insert double-leg mounted greenery

Fig. 7.10
Bend
into position

Fig. 7.12
Positioning the inner edge pieces in the moss

Fig. 7.13   The side view

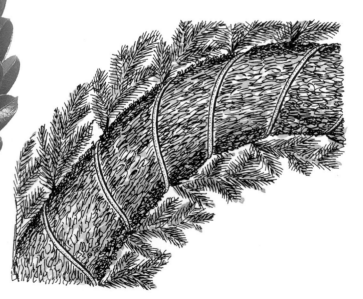

Plate 24   Foliage based chaplet

Fig. 7.14   The appearance of the mossed frame with the edging completed

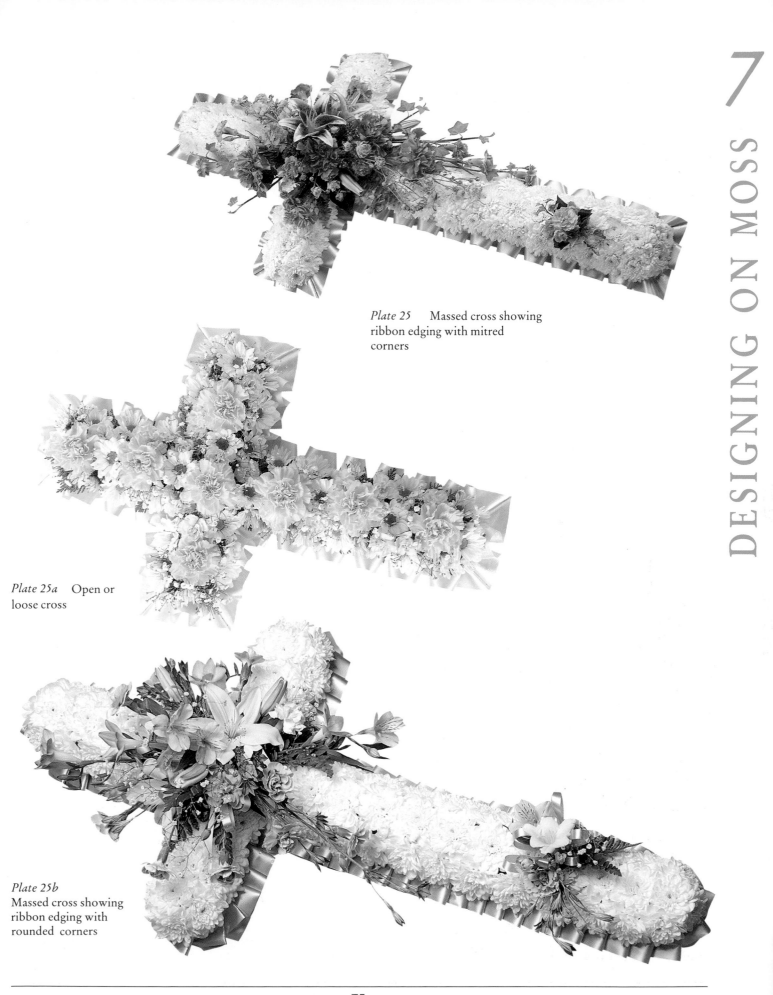

Plate 25   Massed cross showing
ribbon edging with mitred
corners

Plate 25a   Open or
loose cross

Plate 25b
Massed cross showing
ribbon edging with
rounded corners

Flower placement

Foliage placement

METHOD

Mount the flowers for the inner and outer edges of the design, using wires of appropriate weight eg. 20 g (0.90 mm) × 7" (180 mm). Position them, making sure that the wires are firmly anchored to the moss base.
If necessary, support wire any of the flower material to be used; for example: Roses 24 g (0.56 mm) × 7" (180 mm). Carnations 22 g (0.71 mm) × 7" (180 mm).

Having obtained the width of the design, the central flowers can be cut, mounted and positioned to achieve the required dome shape. Keeping within this outline, the remaining flowers can be placed into the areas at different levels to create interest and recession (*Fig. 7.15*).

Whatever method is used, either placement with the flower material or after, the foliage must be contained within the design and must not 'take over'.

The cheaper foliage can be used to mask the moss base, and the more expensive foliage 'patterned' throughout the design, taking care that all material is placed firmly in the moss (*Fig. 7.16*).

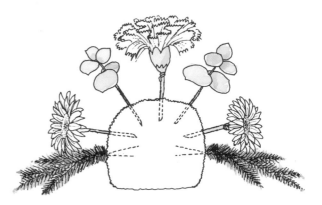

Fig. 7.16

Spray design when completed with water mister.

Mount the protected card with a taped or green stub wire carefully in one corner (single-leg mount), push into moss and return end securely back into the underside of the frame. The placing of the card is of the utmost importance and should be positioned so as to be read easily.

Fig. 7.15

Presentation

The shop forecourt

Presentation starts in front of the window.

If your shop displays flowers and plants on the forecourt, it is essential that they are presented well. Attractively wrapped, quality flowers, clearly priced and well set out in front of the shop can increase overall sales, encourage impulse buying and entice new customers.

Outside displays must be limited to your own forecourt within the bounds of local bye-laws and pedestrian safety. It is the responsibility of the boss to ensure that the display stand is constructed safely and securely, perhaps using purpose-built stands which are now on the market. Thereafter, the maintenance of a clean, fresh, tidy, frontage is the duty of the staff.

It takes self discipline to ensure that the forecourt display is checked frequently, tidied and replenished with price tickets on the correct items (customers do tend to move them) and that the plants are watered.

Suitable flowers for outside sale are mixed bunches of, for instance, spray carnations and spray chrysanthemums, at various prices; any other tolerant flowers according to the season; or flowers reflecting a good market purchase.

Outside prices must be competitive.

Flower bunches should be attractively wrapped in water repellent cellophane, protected from damage and easy to pick up in order to encourage impulse sales. Initial impulse sales from the forecourt may lead to larger sales. Be alert to the chance of enlarging such sales. Customers often ask 'What will go with this?' If they don't, you can enquire if they wish to add further flowers to the bunch, thus increasing the sale.

Outdoor seasonal plants and tolerant house plants look attractive and sell from the forecourt. Do not put out delicate plants in a sharp wind. At all costs avoid putting out plants which are past their best. They downgrade the whole display.

The overall image of your forecourt must be colourful and arresting.

The ultimate test of any display is the sales it produces.

Window display

The bold presentation of fresh flowers, healthy plants and interesting sundries in a clean, well-lit shop window attracts passers-by and entices them into the shop. It is silent selling.

The window needs to be changed frequently, even daily. A changing window reassures people that the flower stock is fresh and freshness is an important factor contributing to the good image of a florist.

Your window is like a flower arrangement. It needs colour, impact, variety, interest, height and a focal point. It must be eye catching.

Window items should be:

- priced to reassure the customer who has a spending limit and because it is now a legal requirement;
- for the enjoyment of passers by; and
- have some large, choice floristry designs.

Larger designs may lead to sales of similar items on a smaller scale and they may be exactly what someone is looking for to place in an office or hotel.

Large planted bowl designs can be both attractive and economical. If the plants are arranged in moss, keep them in their pots so that they can be easily returned to stock. Use your window to sell ideas.

Whilst you are arranging your window, go outside frequently to assess the effect you are creating. Is it attractive when viewed from the pavement? Is the pricing clear?

A well-lit window at night can encourage many extra sales when people are just window shopping. So, at the end of the day make sure the window is showing a full and interesting display.

Promote the relay service in your window, but do not obscure the view with posters. Leave a clear view into the shop. People enjoy watching florists at work.

Throughout the day you must maintain a full and tidy display. Whenever a sale is made from the window the item must be replaced or the window rearranged. The window glass must be kept clean inside and out and the base of the window display kept clean and free from damaged leaves and other rubbish.

Specially designed window displays can promote a theme, a subject, topical comments or even a single product. They need to be well thought out but not work-intensive. If you get known for attractive windows people will go out of their way to see and enjoy what you have done.

Inside shop display

Your shop must be kept clean. The floor must be clear of obstacles, clean and dry to avoid accidents to customers and staff.

Always keep a clean, dry, wrapping surface ready for business. Practical equipment should be to hand; paper, Sellotape, ribbon, cut flower and plant food and care leaflets. Have a clean order taking area with a selection of gift and sympathy cards, selection guides, directories and an ample supply of order pads and pens.

Posters and banners displayed at eye level can speed order taking.

Every item in the shop should be priced.

Flowers inside the shop must be fresh, in clean vases of fresh water to which flower food has been added and displayed so that they have room to breathe and damage is kept to a minimum. They must be kept well within reach of the sales florist when selling from the display. Flowers grouped in varieties, complementary varieties, or by colour, make it easier for the customer to choose and for you, the florist, to sell.

Plants in the shop should be grouped for maximum selling impact, but remember they like light and hate draughts.

Foliage plants with a longer shelf life can be placed where they will continue to thrive, yet be immediately available to customers. Bright flowering plants, grouped together, draw attention to themselves and sell quickly in a good selling position.

Expensive flowering plants, like stephanotis and gardenias, need the best conditions and the very best sales pitch to ensure speedy sales.

Give attention to stock rotation.

Your shop is a stage, give a first class, professional performance everytime

Plate 26   Cushion heart

Sundries need not occupy a top sales area, but they should not be left in the same place too long. Moving them stimulates fresh interest. Pottery and shelves must be clean and sundries used in the window must be washed before being returned to the shelves.

The sales florist

You and your stock must create a good first impression. Customer confidence starts with presentation, not only of your stock, but of yourself. A well groomed personal appearance, a welcoming smile and clear speech all give the impression of efficiency, care and attention.

Clothes should be comfortable and warm and it is wise to wear sensible shoes both for comfort and safety. An overall or tabard will protect your own clothing and project your shop's corporate image by the use of 'house colours'.

When there are no customers about the sales florist must not disappear into the workroom. There is work to do. No customers will walk into a dead shop and the flowers will not wait for next week's sale. So change the display and keep busy. Customers are curious. They will come in to see what you are doing and then buy.

The shop is a stage. You set it and you take a leading part. Give a first class performance every time.

Cash and carry sales

Knowledge

Florists cannot afford to have indifferent sales people on the shop floor. Neither is the sales area the place for a trembling beginner who has been thrown in at the deep end. A sales florist has to feel confident before a good sale can be made. Knowledge gives that confidence.

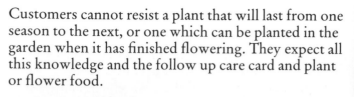

A beginner could take on the flower bunches and the single plants first. Establish a pleasant relationship with the customer. Be seen to wrap flowers and handle money competently. Gradually take on the more difficult situations that need specialised knowledge, like flower arrangements, sympathy designs and relay orders.

A sales florist must be fully aware of the stock, stock rotation, prices and general availability. Otherwise, that florist is incompetent in front of a customer.

Selling presents a golden opportunity to exploit a good market buy, that is when a quantity of quality flowers has been bought at a low price. To a customer who has expressed no preferences these flowers should be your first and immediate recommendation. It is profitable for the business.

To the customer who has no preference, sell the quality flowers of which you have a good stock. Never sell the last twenty yellow carnations if there are two hundred magnificent pale pink ones in the building.

Never sell poor material. Put the decision firmly on the boss: 'I do not think these flowers are fit for sale. I would not like my mother to buy them'. The boss can then make the decision.

Tender flowers, such as sweet peas, which have a short vase life, must be sold quickly if they are to be profitable.

Customers cannot resist a plant that will last from one season to the next, or one which can be planted in the garden when it has finished flowering. They expect all this knowledge and the follow up care card and plant or flower food.

A sales florist is expected to advise on flower choice for special occasions, colour co-ordination, design and suitability. Frequently on the shop floor the florist has to put together decorative plants that will do well in a customer's specific location and explain the reasons for their recommendations as they sell.

This knowledgeable service separates the specialist florist from the flower seller.

Sales florists must be sensitive to every situation and always alert to the customer who wants something different and is ready to pay for imaginative advice and skill. Rise to the challenge.

It is the sales florist's knowledge and the way it is put over that gives the customer confidence and increases the money in the till.

Good sales mean good pay days.

Customers welcome information on the lasting qualities of flowers and their unseen advantages, for example, the gradual opening up of freesias, and the way their fragrance is enhanced in a warm room.

Communication

Be aware of your customers immediately they enter the shop and build up your picture of them. Recognise different types of customer – the business man; the older person; the happy present buyer. Communicate with them in the appropriate way.

Create a good impression. It is important that the customer likes the way you look, move, stand and smile, the tone of your voice and your eye contact with them. A positive attitude reassures them that you are intelligent and efficient.

Clearly expressed information and advice are expected from a sales florist. Turn your face to the customer when you speak. Make sure every word you say is heard and understood. Express yourself sensibly and fairly slowly. Eliminate habits of speech like 'sort of', 'you know' and 'I mean'.

Build up a wide vocabulary that will improve your communication with customers, for example, 'sturdy', 'glossy', 'structure', 'trailing', 'vertical'. Stand still. Look into your customer's face and let the customer look at you. Learn about them. Listen and show real interest. Concentrate on what the customer is saying and start to relate it to the service your shop offers.

Through careful and courteous questions, identify the customer's needs. Think quickly, avoid being long winded, understand, recommend, advise and offer alternatives. Your attitude will increase the customer's interest and improve the sale.

The sales florist transforms the customer's hopes and wishes into a tangible product, selling and showing exquisite flowers with charm and understanding. It is absolutely essential that the challenge of a luxury sale is recognised and dealt with to the complete satisfaction and confidence of the customer.

Cash and carry flower sales

Wrapping up one or two bunches of flowers that the customer has chosen themselves is very easy. Selling a beautiful gift of flowers for a customer to carry away, while that customer watches you, listens and waits is a task calling for knowledge and speed.

Enquire if the flowers are a present or a personal buy, thus learning the occasion and reason for the purchase. Ask the customer's colour preference.

Never ask, 'How much do you want to spend?' Estimate in your head a good price for the situation and begin to build a lovely flower gift in your hand. Select choice flowers with tall, strong stems first.

Then, whilst you hold them, create the beautiful arrangement that the customer really wants.

Consult and please your customer all the time as you put together colour, perfume and varieties of shape which your knowledge tells you will be popular with your customer. From time to time give an indication of the price the purchase has reached.

Having advised well and displayed the flowers, bring the sale to a close, saying, perhaps, 'Would you prefer more carnations or extra roses?' Wrap the flowers to protect them against damage and include a care card and flower food.

Be seen to add up correctly. Show that you are efficient at the till. Give the correct change.

Hand the flowers over in a way that is most comfortable for the customer. Smile. Warn against damage and reassure your customer that the choice has been wise.

Tidy and refill vases, pick up any leaves and wipe the wrapping surface.

Cash and carry plant sales

You must know the condition of every plant in your shop and groom them daily. Unhappy plants create an impression of carelessness and on seeing them, customers become wary of purchasing anything at all.

Do not lose money on plants by letting them deteriorate. If one looks poor, speak to the boss and move the indifferent plant from the display into a special price area. It will be given a good home by a plant lover who knows its worth.

A customer would like a plant. Enquire if it is for a present or for the home. Is a flowering or a green plant wanted? (See Plate 27.)

Sell your best plants first. Lift the plants gently and display them to the customer. Be seen to appreciate them. Offer two or three alternative plants and varieties. Customers like to hold the plant themselves. Say why the plants you offer will be a good purchase. Give advice on their care.

If a customer has a special place in mind for a house plant, listen and advise on size, shape and tolerance to light and temperature. Insist that no flowering or variegated plant will tolerate poor light, draught or extremes of temperature.

Sell a pot cover to complete a gift. This is essential if it is going to a hospital. (See Plate 28.)

Wrap the plant to protect against damp and chill. Include a care card and plant food.

Further sales could include a watering can, sprayer and a plant book. All of them are invaluable in the home.

Cash and carry sundries

The range of sundries a florist stocks is decided by the boss. He/she takes into consideration the location of the shop, local customer spending power and the shop space available for a profitable display.

Sundries can be divided roughly into two groups:

- those which are incorporated into a plant or flower order, such as ribbons, silk and dried flowers, pot covers and baskets, candles and balloons, and

- those which have nothing to do with flowers and plants. These vary from fine porcelain to novelty gift ware. Diversification into this area can be profitable. However, their long life should not result in customer boredom. Inexpensive items and buyer's mistakes should be moved as sales items.

The boss who stocks expensive breakables will provide safe shelving and well-lit display areas. Thereafter the sales florist is responsible for safety, cleanliness, pricing and changing the display frequently.

A knowledge of colour, texture, shape and proportion makes it easy for a florist to sell pot covers and flower containers. A plant in peak condition, displayed in a well proportioned china or pottery cover, subtly colour blended, will sell as a complete item before the day is out.

Fresh, dried or silk-polyester flower arrangements in well designed, textured containers will undoubtedly sell if they are on show. One may even sell the single container and foam once the customer has got the idea of how to use them. Dried and silk-polyester flowers and foliage are a profitable standard sundries item. When learning to display, it is wise to separate them from each other, for their texture and character are quite different. Dried materials look well in rough textured baskets, while silk-polyester material, grouped in colours, can hang, massed, from the ceiling like chandeliers or climb up a trellised wall.

The display of silk-polyester material has to be disciplined or it can demand more space than its profitability justifies.

A stock of good sundries will encourage customers to browse and feel at home. Whether sold as additions to flower sales or by themselves, sundries put money in the till and are a constant challenge to the sales florist who wants his/her sales record to be the best.

Written orders

Knowledge

Before taking written orders you must have the basic knowledge needed for cash and carry sales plus a specialist knowledge of:

1 Funeral floristry

2 Flower arranging with fresh, dried and silk-polyester materials, with or without accessories

3 Economic pricing of make-up work

4 The delivery policy of your shop

5 The relay system

6 Selection guides, banners and special items

7 The system for accepting credit cards and cheques in your shop

8 Your system for filing order papers and accounts in your shop

9 The economy in time and profitability of a clearly written order.

Information

Orders for your own shop and for relay need the same basic information:

1 Full name and address of the customer placing the order, and their telephone number

2 Full name and address of the recipient and their telephone number, where it may assist delivery

3 Day and date of delivery

4 Cost of delivery

5 Flowers requested and their cost

6 Card message or the customer's own card

7 Transmission and service charge, if any

8 Method of payment – cash, cheque or credit card.

Writing

To do their jobs properly, other people have to be able to read and understand what you have written. These include:

1 The customer

2 Order packer

Plate 27 Display of foliage plants

3 Driver

4 The florist who transmits the order

5 Make up florist

6 Accounts clerk

Learn how to take a sensible written order

When discussing the order with the customer, check, at the outset, if the order can be delivered at all.

Lead your customer through the routine of giving an order so that you get the information you want in the sequence you want it.

Use a professional florist's vocabulary and learn to spell such words as director, colleague and courageous. Ask customers to spell unusual surnames, house, road and place names. Be interested and enthusiastic. Get the facts right.

Know the flowers and plants that are available and work your way to a sensible order, preferably unspecified, that can be executed well. Think about the implications as you ask the occasion or purpose for gift flowers. 'Does your friend like all flowers?' 'Any special colours?' 'Shall we choose a lovely selection of fresh flowers that go well together?'

Write down a full, clear statement of all that you agree with your customer so that everyone can read your writing and understand what you have written.

If a customer is adamant that certain flowers are wanted, check that they will be available before promising anything. Try to get a second or third choice. Use the word 'some' rather than specify a particular quantity of flowers, if possible.

At all times avoid antagonising the buyer, order packer, the workroom, the driver or your fellow members of staff with impossible requests that could have been avoided.

Understand what is involved in producing specific make-up items; the quantity and availability of the flowers needed and the viability of the order in terms of time and money. Guide your customer to choose an effective design that will both please and yet be practical and profitable for the workroom to make. If you ever feel that you are getting out of your depth consult a senior member of staff. This can be done without loss of dignity on your part and without diminishing the customer's confidence in you.

Gift and sympathy flowers always have an accompanying message. Get it right, spell it correctly and read it back to your customer. The message is as important as the flowers.

A card in the customer's own handwriting must never be separated from its order paper. It should be keyed by recording the order number discreetly on the back of the card. The card should then be inserted into a cellophane sleeve or shop envelope and attached to its order paper. Never put a pin through the card itself. Faultless card drill must be followed. For instance:

- Complete the written order form with figures and correct addition.
- Have the order checked by a senior.
- Follow your shop drill for till recording the cash, cheque or credit card received in payment.
- Give the correct change and receipts.
- Alert the buyer if specified flowers are needed.
- File the order paper in its correct place.

Taking a written order for the future delivery of the flowers is a great moment of trust. The customer knows what is wanted, is about to part with the money and yet cannot see what it is that they have bought.

Gift flowers, plants or arrangements, delivered to the door in a smart van, are prestige presents. Very, very few people expect their gift to be on the cheap. So, understand their expectations and sell them their dreams. Minimum prices have nothing to do with it.

When talking to your customer, stand so that the customer is looking at a beautiful display of fresh flowers all the time.

Show the Selection Guide; point out the posters and banners. Your customer can then browse, study the prices and decide. Very often, a satisfactory agreement is reached after you have explained that the lowest price on the illustration buys a smaller version and that the designs can be made in different colours.

Selling from pictures is easy for the sales florist but does not suit every situation. Customers want you to understand their special need, whether it be for a gift costing ten pounds or two hundred. They want your knowledge, your voice and your advice.

Learn how to offer a range of prices:

'A pleasing bouquet of fresh flowers, gift wrapped, costs around "A" pounds, "B" pounds or "C" pounds'.
'If you would like a wider selection of choice flowers, you must spend around "D" pounds or "E" pounds'.

'If you have something smaller in mind, why not have a small bunch of fresh flowers in a plain wrap?'

Give the customers time to listen and decide. Discuss the words and prices to be used in your shop. Practise them to yourself on the bus, in the car or as you walk to work. They will come out beautifully at the right moment and not sound forced.

Pricing family sympathy flowers is a sensitive situation. Listen and understand exactly what your customer wants. Help the customers with advice, interpret their needs in flowers and ask a proper price.

There must never be heartbreak and disappointment at the funeral service because you failed to give the right advice and state the correct price for what the customer had in mind.

Customers do not know what they are asking for in terms of flower availability or price. A cross of all red roses that the customer yearns for, cannot always be afforded. A cross of red carnations or a pure white cross with a spray of red roses become equally appreciated when offered sympathetically. They may also fall within the customer's price range.

Lovely funeral flowers that linger in the memory are those which have been sold imaginatively and at a price that has ensured skilled workmanship and a beautiful design.

In design work, you must charge enough to do a decent job. Good workmanship must be charged for if it is to cover training, skilled experience, time spent on the design and provide a contribution to the profits of the whole business.

Telephone sales

Selling on the telephone is the same as selling in the shop, only you have to listen harder, speak even more clearly and use a wider vocabulary. Your customer cannot see you. Your voice, manner and words are the only contact.

In a clear, confident voice, identify your shop. Speak slowly. Listen. When you can, politely, take charge of the conversation. Ask your customer's name, address and telephone number. Ask questions that will give you all the information you will need, in the order you want it. Ask that awkward names be spelt. Ask how payment is to be made: cheque, credit card or a personal call into the shop.

The customer cannot see what is being bought, so it is up to you to recommend. Phrase your recommendations in simple, descriptive words that conjure up a mental picture. Talk, for instance, of long stemmed carnations, soft pinks, dark green foliage, trailing plants. Use the word 'fresh', never use 'nice'.

Recognise the level of gift your customer wants. Know how you are going to discriminate in words between a small, average and big flower gift. Quote a sensible price. On the phone it is essential to quote a price high enough to make absolutely sure your customer will not be disappointed with the size of the product.

Always read the complete order back to the customer, including the method of payment, slowly and clearly. Put your all into your voice and see if you can get the customer to say, 'Thank you. That was lovely'. Fully complete the written order. File papers in the correct place.

Delivery information

The van and driver are, probably, the most expensive bit of equipment in the shop and must be used economically.

Write addresses clearly so that the driver can read them. It is time wasting, aggravating and totally uneconomic for a driver to go up and down a road trying to find a badly written or carelessly taken address. Likewise do not accept a house name only. Ask for a house number in the road.

Get a description of the location. Take the recipient's phone number. Never ask 'When would you like the flowers delivered?' You are inviting your customer to reply, 'Now, this very minute.' Ask 'Would you like your flowers delivered tomorrow or is there a special date for delivery?' Thus, deliveries become orderly, not instant.

Learn the skill of avoiding a.m. or p.m. deliveries. Only funeral flowers, ship and airport arrivals and departures automatically demand a specific time. Timed gift deliveries are uneconomic in terms of drivers' time and vehicle running costs. Consider your driver's safety. Timed deliveries in different directions cause stress to the driver and increase the risk of an accident.

If an awkward timed delivery is unavoidable, offer delivery by taxi. The customer is usually very willing to pay the additional cost.

If a delivery is to be to a named ship, the driver must know the surname, first name, home address, class, deck and cabin numbers and the sailing time.

Plate 28 Selection
of pot covers

For deliveries to an airport the driver must know the surname, and first name, home address, airline flight number, destination and the time of arrival or departure, whichever applies.

Hospital addresses must be detailed and accurate. These days drivers are being asked to deliver to wards. This is an enormously extravagant use of the driver's time. Address mistakes for the floating hospital population must be eliminated by the florist at the point of sale. The driver has to know the patient's surname, first name, home address and telephone number so that the patient can be quickly identified in a busy hospital.

Florists must look after their drivers. There is potential stress everywhere; in town, in traffic jams and high rise flats; in the country, in narrow lanes and from dawdling holiday makers.

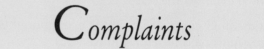

Complaints

No customer will complain unless it is felt to be justified. Stay calm, alert and listen. It may be upsetting but you must not show it. Listen. Do not bristle. Do not make it a confrontation. You may be in the wrong. Be sympathetic, 'I am so sorry you were disappointed.' Find the order work paper. The written word establishes facts.

At your first problem, get management help *immediately*.

The shop must be seen as first class, efficient and caring. A complaint is a management situation. Customers like it that way. Complete customer satisfaction has to be reached.

Dissatisfaction perpetuated is disastrous for business. Afterwards, review the nature of the complaint, and the part played in it by the shop, and plan how that particular mistake can be avoided in the future. Learn from complaints. They clear out an air of self-satisfaction and make the whole shop look again at organisation.

THE TREATMENT, CARE, STORAGE AND AVAILABILITY OF COMMERCIAL FLOWERS

Appendix I   Table 2

	Alstroemeria	Antirrhium	Anemone	Carnation
Availability	Hybrid: April–November Common: July–August	April–June	Late autumn and winter. Available other times, but opens too quickly in hot weather	All year, cheaper in summer
Packing	Boxes – always in bunches, usually of 5	Usually in boxes with stems intertwined	Very tightly in bunches of 10 or more usually mixed colours	In boxes or bunches Any numbers, 20–100
Unpacking & immediate treatment	Cut stems	Cut stems	Cut stems	Cut stems (not at node)
Leaves	Remove lower leaves	Remove lower leaves Very slippery, so sweep up quickly	None	Remove lower leaves
Water	Plenty, but change often as stems can make water smell	Plenty	Plenty, refill daily	Average
Special	Hybrid is a very good laster		Keep out of direct sunlight	Keep out of draught Can go soft in thundery weather
Colour range	Hybrid: mauve, pink, red, yellow, orange Common: yellow, orange only	Full range except blue	Scarlet, purple, puce pink	All except blue, but white ones can be dyed blue
What to look for – good		Good straight stem	Plenty of scarlet in mixed bunches	Strong stems
What to look for – bad	Spotting	Bottom fleurettes falling, leaving the seedbox	Elongated space between flower and green frill (calyx)	Stamens should not be visible Calyx should not be split
Meaning			'Lilies of the field' in the Bible Meaning: refused in love	Red: great admiration White: pure ardent love Yellow: disdain, rejection
Other notes	Useful for pipping and small arrangements		Will not last long in foam	Can be used whole or feathered in corsage and wedding floristry

APPENDIX 1

	Chrysanthemum bloom	Spray AYR (all year round)	Daffodils (Narcissi)	Dahlias
Availability	August–January	All year round	December–April Daffodils start earlier but Narcissi continue longer	July–October (or until frosts)
Packing	In boxes packed at both ends with stems intertwined	Paper covered bundles	Usually bunches of 10	Bunches of 10
Unpacking and immediate treatment	Great care required – crush or split stems	Cut stems	Cut stems These are very slimy, sweep up at once	Cut stems
Leaves	Remove lower leaves	Remove lower leaves	Leaves (spikes) supplied, except with outdoor crop	Remove excess leaves and buds
Water	Plenty warm water if limp	Plenty warm water if limp	Plenty	Plenty, can spray flower with water
Special	Avoid all rough treatment Handle with care or they will shatter	Avoid draughts and direct sunlight		Keep out of direct sunlight
Colour range	White and cream, yellow, gold, brown, bronze, wine red, peach, mauve, purple, pink	As for chrysanthemum bloom	Yellow, white, orange	Very wide range, all except blue
What to look for – good	Strong stems, tight centre, unblemished leaves	Strong stems, plenty of bloom	Usually bought 'goose necked' when bud has just turned over	Strong stems
What to look for – bad	Back petals drooping Yellow centre showing Mark on leaves (In reflex varieties petals do curl back naturally)	Centre flowers too open Back petals soft and drooping	Split stem ends	Back petals drooping or damaged
Meaning	Red: I love White: truth Yellow: slighted love		Holy flower, symbol of Easter Narcissus: egotism	
Other notes	Very long lasting, but leaves die first so sell some foliage with them	Useful for based wreaths, crosses, cushions, hearts	Throw away daffodil water after use	Not a long lasting flower. Good for decoration and wreath work, but not for presents

	Delphinium	Euphorbia	Freesia (single)	Freesia (double)
Availability	June, July and August Blue bee available longer	Winter	Mainly October–April Always available but not good in hot weather	Mainly spring
Packing	Bunches of 5–10	Usually bunches of 10	Bunches 5–10, usually in polythene wrapping	Bunches
Unpacking and immediate treatment	Cut stems	Cut stems	Cut stems	Cut stems
Leaves	Remove lower leaves	Remove lower leaves	None	None
Water	Plenty	Plenty	Plenty	Plenty
Special	Keep out of direct sunlight		Avoid direct sunlight Remove bottom flower if 'crinkled'	
Colour range	All shades of blue, white, pink (rare)	Scarlet (orangey) white	Very wide range Sold in mixed bunches in UK	Cream, white and mauve only
What to look for – good	Strong stems		Strong straight stems	Smooth petals
What to look for – bad	Lower fleurettes dropping	Crisping of leaves	Lower flowers crinkle	Crinkly flowers
Meaning				
Other notes		Very graceful	Do not leave in polythene wrap too long or flowers will 'sweat'	

APPENDIX 1

APPENDIX 1

	Gentian	Gerbera	Gladioli	Hyacinth (cut)
Availability	Autumn and spring	All year round but best in spring Not very good in hot weather	All year round due to importation, but best in August–September	Mid-November to April
Packing	Bunches	Boxed in colours	Bunches of 5–10	Bunches
Unpacking and immediate treatment	Cut stems	Cut stems	Cut stems	Cut stems Sweep up at once as they are very slimy
Leaves	None	None	Strip off a few outer leaves	Usually supplied with leaves
Water	Warm water	Not too much	Plenty warm water if required to open	Plenty, but watch lower flowers
Special	These open in sunlight and tend to close up at night	Not very good in foam	Fleurettes will open all up stem	
Colour range	Blue	Very wide range	Very wide range Colours limited out of season	Mainly white and pink Blue, mauve, red, yellow 'straw' and apricot are limited
What to look for – good	Flowers a good clear blue	Good strong stems	Strong, straight stems	
What to look for – bad	Moulding, dampness, crinkling	Moulding at centre	Rusting on leaves	Petals going transparent
Meaning			Ready armed	Sport Purple: sorrow White: unobtrusive loveliness
Other notes		Native of South Africa	Good for large church decoration	Very useful as pipping for wedding and corsage work

	Iris	Lilac	Lily of the Valley	Lilies
Availability	All year round	December–May	On root available all year round Frame: April Outdoor: May	See Appendix 1 table 3
Packing	Bunches of 5–10	Bunches of 10	Bunches of 10	
Unpacking and immediate treatment	Cut stems, removing blanched portion	Crush stems, strip off bark at base of stem	Cut stems, throw away roots	
Leaves	Sometimes a few outer leaves to be removed	None In the case of outdoor local lilac, remove all leaves	Apple green Outdoor frame: darker green	
Water	Plenty	Plenty of warm water	Plenty	
Special	Avoid direct sunlight	Lilac is a bit tricky but will normally last well in water Not foam	White	
Colour range	Mainly deep and medium blue Also yellow, white, cream, purple, all limited out of season	White, mauve, purple	Strong stems	
What to look for – good	Good firm stems		Top flowers should not be fully out	
What to look for – bad	Rusting on leaves Secondary bud is not an advantage			
Meaning	Valour, wisdom	White: humility, innocence Purple: first emotion of love	Humility and purity Tears of Virgin Mary	
Other notes	If bought in bud, this will come out beautifully If open, damage to petals likely		Very strong perfume	

APPENDIX 1

	Mimosa	Orchids	Paeonies	Poinsettia
Availability	December–March	Mostly all year due to importation Cattleya Cymbidium Phalenopsis Odonotoglossum Dendrobium	June	Winter
Packing	Bunches	Individually, stems of 3–20 Varieties listed above: stems often in test tubes	Bunches of 5–10	Singly in boxes, about 25 stems intertwined
Unpacking and immediate treatment	Crush stems	Cut stems	Crush stems	Cut stems
Leaves		None	Remove lower leaves	Remove lower leaves
Water	Plenty	Average	Plenty, refill daily	Plenty Warm
Special	Avoid direct heat or sunlight			Avoid draughts
Colour range	Yellow	Purple, yellow, white. Pink, cream, green, gold. White. White, purple, yellow, orange Purple	White, pink, deep red	Scarlet, pink, greeny white
What to look for – good	Fluffy fleurettes	Strong and fleshy	Buy in bud (but not too tight) as they open very quickly	Good clear colour
What to look for – bad	Browning or hardening of flowers. Distinguish between buds & dead flowers	Brown marks on edge of petals	If buds are too tight, they may never open Watch for browning (damping)	Damage to coloured bracts Curling of leaves
Meaning	Daintiness		Bashfulness	
Other notes	Two kinds	Should last well if not bruised.	Sarah Bernhardt (pale pink) – best variety to be marketed	Small yellow flowers found in the centre of the coloured bracts

	Roses	Scabious	Stephanotis	Stock
Availability	All year	Summer	Mainly summer but about May–November	Spring and early summer
Packing	Bunches of 10–20 or boxes of 20–50 according to size and length of stem	Bunches of 10	Punnets or cellophane bags of 10 or 25	Tall: in boxes with stems intertwined Mid and short, bunches of 3–5, often with root
Unpacking and immediate treatment	Cut stems Remove thorns by machine, scissors or knife	Cut stems	Stems are very short, so only cut off a tiny bit, spray lightly	Cut stems
Leaves	Remove lower leaves	Remove lower leaves		Remove lower leaves
Water	Plenty of warm water if required to open	Plenty, this will smell if left too long	Can immerse but not for too long	Plenty, but not to cover leaves
Special				If stored too long they become blue and slimy, making water smell
Colour range	Very wide range, except blue Mauve is scarce	Mauve/blue Other colours grown in gardens but not usually marketed	White only	White, mauve, pink, deep red, cream, salmon pink
What to look for – good	Good shape, strong straight stems	Centre should be green and firm	Clear white, no bruising	Strong stems, good leaves
What to look for – bad	Rusting on leaves Blueing of pink and red roses Outer petals damaged	If stamens are showing they are too advanced to sell Rusting on leaves	Black pollen showing on petals	Blueing of flowers Lower fleurettes should be perfect
Meaning	Red: great love White: charm, innocence Yellow: jealousy	Unfortunate love		Lasting beauty
Other notes	Miniature roses very long lasting		Excellent wedding and corsage work	

APPENDIX 1

	Sweet Pea	Tulips	Violets
Availability	April (scarce) May, June	Mid-December to May Outdoor only in May	October–April
Packing	Bunches of 10	Bunches of 5	Bunched
Unpacking and immediate treatment	Cut stems	Cut stems, condition well to ensure straightness	Cut stems and spray flowers with water
Leaves	None Try to sell some foliage with them	Remove lower leaves	Keep with bunches Sometimes ivy leaves are used
Water	Plenty	Thirsty drinkers To be placed in not more than 6″ (150 mm) water	Plenty
Special		Opens very quickly in direct sunlight Flowers will develop and stems lengthen in water	Flowers take water through heads so can be sprayed or immersed in water
Colour range	As stock, but also scarlet	All except blue and there is one nearly black	Purple Herricks (no smell) Princess of Wales (smell) White very rare
What to look for – good	Strong stems, 4 or more fleurettes on each	Firm stem Clean foliage	
What to look for – bad	Blueing or spotting	'Spot' (like measles) 'Water stem' (part of stem goes transparent no water passes through). Should not occur from reliable nurseries	
Meaning	Delicate pleasure	Red: love Striped: beautiful eyes Yellow: hopeless love	
Other notes			Parma violet: double and paler is very rare, almost extinct

Appendix 1   Table 3

Flower	Arum	Auratum	Longiflorum	Nerine
Availability	Mainly spring but obtainable at other times	Late spring and possibly summer	Mainly spring and summer, but obtainable all year	Autumn and winter
Packing	Boxes according to size of flowers	Bunches	Bunches	Bunches of 10
Unpacking and immediate treatment	Cut stems	Cut stems	Cut stems	Cut stems
Leaves		Remove lower leaves	Remove lower leaves	None
Water	Plenty Refill daily	Plenty Refill daily	Plenty Refill daily	Average
Special		Brown stamens will stain and should be removed as flowers open	Yellow stamens should be removed as flowers open	Rare scarlet one is 'fluorescent' and smells of chocolate
Colour range	Pink, white, yellow	Creamy white	White	Mainly pink, scarlet – rare, salmon pink, white
What to look for – good	Freshly cut arums are cream on outside	Very tight buds	Good firm buds and foliage	
What to look for – bad	Pollen on stamens Crinkly at tip		Splitting of flowers as they open, droopy leaves	
Meaning	Ardour, zeal			
Other notes		Very large, flowers	Usually sold by flower not by stem	Useful for wedding work

Flower	Rubrum	Tiger and various orange and yellow lilies. Royal Gold	Valotta or Jersey Lily
Availability	Late summer and throughout winter	Mainly summer	Summer
Packing	Bunches	Bunches	Bunches of 10
Unpacking and immediate treatment	Cut stems	Cut stems	Cut stems
Leaves	Remove lower leaves	Remove lower leaves	None
Water	Plenty Refill daily	Plenty Refill daily	Average
Special	Brown stamens should be removed	Brown or yellow stamens should be removed as flower opens	
Colour range	White, with red blotch	Orange, brown, yellow	Orangey red
What to look for – good			
What to look for – bad	Crinkly petals	Crinkly petals	
Meaning		Yellow, gaiety	
Other notes			

Appendix 1   Table 4

	Eucalyptus	Grevillea	Pittosporum
Availability	Mainly October–April Various kinds	Mainly November–February	October–April Available at other times but top leaves too young to last
Packing	Large bunches	Large bunches	Large bunches
Unpacking and immediate treatment	Crush stems	Crush stems	Crush stems
Leaves			
Water	Plenty Refill daily	Plenty	Plenty
Special	Can be 'glycerined'	Can be 'glycerined' Obtainable dyed in various colours	Can be 'glycerined'
Colour range	Grey-green	Green with silver back, red stems	Light green
What to look for – good			
What to look for – bad	Drying off		Flagging of top leaves Drying off

Many other varieties of foliage will be used, too many to mention, but the main principles – crushing the stems and providing plenty of water – apply to all, as many have woody stems and all are very 'thirsty'.

Appendix 2   Table 5

Name	Origin	Classification	Conditions	Care
Adiantum (Maidenhair Fern)	Brazil	Difficult	Draught-free Partial shade Pure air	Water: Winter – sparingly Summer – freely Spray leaves
Asparagus Plumosus	South Africa	Easy	Normal	Water: Winter – sparingly Summer – freely Feed: March–October Spray leaves
Begonia Rex	China India South America	Delicate	Pure air Partial shade	Water: Winter – sparingly Summer – freely Feed: March–October Keep water off the leaves
Fatshedera Lizei	France	Easy	Winter – cool	Water: Winter – sparingly Summer – freely Feed: March–October Leaves – spray clean

TRAILING PLANTS

Name	Origin	Classification	Conditions	Care
Chlorophytum	South Africa	Easy	Light Tolerates gas	Water: Winter – sparingly Summer – freely Feed: March–October Spray leaves
Hedera **H. Helix Chicago** **H. Helix Lutzii** **H. Helix Glacier**	Asia Europe Africa Canary Islands	Easy	Light Moist Steady temperature	Water: Winter – sparingly Summer – freely Feed: March–October Leaves – spray clean
Tradescantia **(Wandering Jew)**	South America	Easy	Light Moist Cool	Water: Winter – sparingly Summer – freely Feed: March–October Leaves – spray clean

APPENDIX 2

CLIMBING PLANTS

Appendix 2   Table 7

APPENDIX 2

Name	Origin	Classification	Conditions	Care
Cissus Antarctica (Kangaroo Vine)	Australia	Easy	Light Moist Tolerates gas Cool	Water: Winter – sparingly Summer – freely Feed: Summer Leaves – spray clean
Hedera Canariensis Variegata	Asia Europe Africa Canary Islands	Easy	Light Moist Steady temperature	Water: Winter – sparingly Summer – freely Feed: March–Oct Leaves – spray clean
Philodendron Scandens (Sweetheart Vine)	Tropical America West Indies	Easy	Shade Draught-free Steady temperature	Water: Winter – sparingly Summer – freely Feed: March–Oct Leaves – spray clean
Rhoicissus Rhomboidea (Grape Vine)	South Africa	Easy	Light Moist	Water: Winter – sparingly Summer – freely Feed: Summer Leaves – spray clean
Ficus Robusta (Rubber Plant)	Australia New Zealand Asia	Easy	Draught-free Cool steady temperature Light	Water: Winter – sparingly Summer – freely Feed: March–Oct Leaves – spray clean
Monstera Deliciosa (Swiss Cheese Plant)	Mexico	Easy	Winter – warmth Draught-free Moist	Water: Winter – sparingly Summer – freely Feed: Summer Leaves – spray clean
Peperomia P. Magnoliae folia P. Caperata P. Hederaefolia	Brazil	Intermediate	Winter–warm Draught-free Light	Water: Winter and summer carefully Leaves – spray
Pilea Cadierei (Aluminium Plant)	South America Indio-China	Intermediate	Draught-free Light/semi-shade Dislikes gas Warmth	Water: Winter and summer (moist) Feed: March–Oct Leaves – spray
Sansevieria (Mother-in-law's Tongue)	South Africa	Easy	Light/semi-shade Dry Steady temperature	Water: Winter – sparingly Summer – carefully Feed: Summer Leaves – spray

Appendix 2   Table 8

Name	Origin	Classific-ation	Availability	Conditions	Care
Achimenes	Tropical America	Intermed-iate	April–June	Light Warmth	Water: Summer – freely Winter – dry Feed: Growing season
Aphelandra (Zebra Plant)	South America	Intermed-iate	April–August	Light Draught-free Warmth Moist	Water: Summer – freely Winter – carefully Feed: Growing season
Astilbe Spiraea	Japan	Easy	May–June	Sunny	Water: Summer – freely
Azalea Indica	Japan	Easy	October–March	Light Draught-free Moist	Water: freely Feed: Flowering season
Begonia (Hybrid)	China India South America	Intermed-iate	March–October	Light Warmth Moist	Water: carefully Spray leaves
Begonia Lorraine – Pink Fireglow-Scarlet	China India South America	Intermed-iate	March–October	Light Warmth Moist	Water: freely Spray leaves
Beloperone (Shrimp Plant)	Mexico	Easy	January–December	Light Sunny Cool	Water: Summer – freely Winter – sparingly Feed: Growing season
Calceolaria	Chile	Easy	December–May	Light Draught-free Moist Cool	Water: carefully Feed: Flowering season

APPENDIX 2

Name	Origin	Classific-ation	Availability	Conditions	Care
Chrysanthemum	Far East	Easy	January–December	Light Draught-free Warmth Moist	Water: Summer – freely Winter – carefully
Cineraria	Canary Islands	Easy	January–May	Light Draught-free Cool	Water: carefully Feed: Flowering season
Cyclamen	Asia Minor	Difficult	July–March	Light Draught-free Humidity Steady temperature	Water: carefully from below, keeping corm dry Pull off dead flowers and leaves
Erica (Heather)	South Africa	Easy	September–March	Light Draught-free Moist Cool	Water: freely in flowering season
Fuchsia	South America	Easy	April–August	Light Moist Cool	Water: Summer – freely Winter – dry Spray leaves
Gloxinia	Brazil	Intermed-iate	May–August	Light Warmth Humidity	Water: carefully Feed: Flowering season
Hyacinth	Europe East Mediterranean	Easy	October–March	Light Cool	Water: carefully Feed: regularly
Hydrangea	Japan	Easy	March–June	Light Draught-free Warmth	Water: freely Feed: occasionally
Impatiens (Busy Lizzie)	Zanzibar	Easy	March–July	Light Warmth	Water: Summer – freely Winter – dry Feed: Growing season

Name	Origin	Classific-ation	Availability	Conditions	Care
Kalanchoe	Madagascar	Easy	January–December	Light Moist Warmth	Water: Freely in flowering season Leaves – spray
Pelargonium Regal	South Africa	Easy	April–July	Sunny Cool in winter	Water: Summer – freely Winter – dry Feed: Growing season
Poinsettia	Mexico	Easy	January–December	Light Draught-free Warmth Moist	Water: carefully Spray leaves occasionally
Primula Obconica	China	Easy	October–May	Light Draught-free Moist Cool	Water: freely Feed: regularly
Saint Paulia (African Violet)	East Africa	Intermed-iate	January–December	Light Draught-free Warmth Moist Steady temperature	Water: freely Feed: During flower season
Solanum (Winter Cherry)	South America	Easy	September–January	Light Moist Cool	Water: carefully Spray leaves Feed: Till berries fallen

APPENDIX 2

About the Contributors

Albert Bailey

Albert studied horticulture at Cheshire College and took a Diploma in Botany and Horticulture at Manchester University. He also studied under Constance Spry. Albert began a business in floristry and horticulture, later going onto gain a teacher's certificate. He ran the first Interflora school in Ireland and taught in the UK and South Africa. He has been an Interflora National Judge and is currently an Interflora Trainer and Assessor.

Ken Neighbour, NSDF

Ken Neighbour is a Past President of the Interflora British Unit and a Past Member of the Interflora World Board. He is a past Chairman of the Interflora Training Commitee and was instrumental in evolving the Interflora Judges' Examination. Ken was an Interflora Trainer for many years and is still a National Verifier for College Courses and an NVQ Trainer.

Irene Bough, NDSF

Irene joined her family's floristry business twenty-five years ago and is now in partnership with her husband and son. A mainstay of Interflora's training team, she is a Trainer, an Assessor and a National Judge for Interflora, as well as being an NVQ Regional Verifier.

Lynda Owen, NSDF

Lynda has been a florist for twenty-five years, and a teacher in further education for ten years. She has been an NVQ Regional Verifier since 1991. Lynda is both a Trainer and a National Judge for Interflora and has also had considerable Interflora competition success. Lynda also won a gold medal and a Ring and Brymer Trophy for the best exhibit by a professional florist at the 1989 Chelsea Flower Show. In 1992 she was one of the designers of the gold medal winning Interflora exhibit at Chelsea, as well as designing the gold medal winning Interflora exhibit at the Hampton Court Show.

Betty Jones, NSDF

Betty has been in the floristy trade for thirty-eight years. She is a Past President and current Council Member of the Society of Floristry. She has won numerous Interflora competition awards and in 1990 and 1992 won gold medals at the Chelsea Flower Show, where she also won the Ring and Brymer Trophy for the best professional floristry exhibit.

Jean Siviter

Jean initially trained as a teacher, but in 1960 bought a small floristry business which she ran for twenty-five years. She was a long-standing Interflora Council Member and served as Chairman of the Education Committee. She was also Chairman of the City and Guilds Floristry Advisory Committee and was awarded an Honorary Membership of the Society of Floristry in recogniton of her work in developing training for florists.